Twintastico Italian Cooking at Home with the Alberti Twins

Twintastico
Italian Cooking at Home with the Alberti Twins

Tony Alberti & John Alberti

PELICAN PUBLISHING COMPANY
Gretna 2019

The word "Pelican" and the depiction of a pelican are trademarks of Pelican Publishing Company, Inc., and are registered in the U.S. Patent and Trademark Office.

Library of Congress Cataloging-in-Publication Data

Names: Alberti, John, 1985- author. | Alberti, Tony, 1985- author.
Title: Twintastico Italian cooking at home with the Alberti Twins.
Description: Gretna : Pelican Publishing Company, 2019. | Includes index.
Identifiers: LCCN 2018023145| ISBN 9781455624430 (pbk. : alk. paper) | ISBN
    9781455624447 (ebook)
Subjects: LCSH: Cooking, Italian--Tuscan style. | LCGFT: Cookbooks.
Classification: LCC TX723.2.T86 .A43 2019 | DDC 641.5945--dc23 LC record
available at https://lccn.loc.gov/2018023145

Printed in China

Published by Pelican Publishing Company, Inc.
1000 Burmaster Street, Gretna, Louisiana 70053
www.pelicanpub.com

To our famiglia, thank you for raising us in a home full of Italian love and passion! We are so blessed and grateful to have a beautiful family. The most important thing in life will always be family. Thank you for making us Italian from our hearts to our stomachs.
Noi ti amiamo più delle parole.

Our Nonna Maria, seated in center with our Mamma on her knee and our Nonno to her right, with family and friends.

Nonna Maria, center, holds her brother Mario with her sisters, Italia to her right and Anna to her left.

Here is our beautiful Nonna Maria in the center. This is our favorite photograph of her—a classic Italian beauty!

To our Nonna Maria, first of all, we want to say *grazie* for everything you have done for us and taught us and continue to teach us. You are the reason we cook and have a passion and love of food. You have showed us the way and we are blessed and grateful to have you as our Nonna. We admire your undeniable strength and courage through the years. You make us so proud of our heritage and culture and being Italian, which will be carried on in our family for generations to come.

Nonna Maria is the oldest of five children, Anna, Italia, Mario, and Angelo. She came from a very small village, high up in the beautiful mountains in the Garfagnana region of Tuscany. She grew up on the family farm and would tell us stories of how she would herd the sheep and how much fun it was on the farm. She loved all the animals.

Nonna, you have taught us so much in life and we admire your lifelong love of Italian food and passion to feed everybody. It is typically Italian, which we adore. We love how you would always say no to water when we asked if you wanted a drink and you would only ever ask for coffee or Vino Rosso, which makes us laugh. Such a Nonna—Nonnas only drink vino and coffee! We get our strength and determination from you. You have created a legacy we are so proud of and it will last forever.

We think back to all the stories you told us about when you came to England in 1950 at the age of twenty and what it was like when you arrived. We will cherish those stories forever. We remember the story you told us of the young English boy next door—a friend of Mamma's—who came into your house one day to find you cooking spaghetti. He immediately ran out at the speed of light, screaming down the street that you were cooking worms. Worms! It still makes us laugh to this day. Back then people had never seen spaghetti, or Italian food for that matter, such as Italian olive oil, coffee, pasta, or wine. It is so hard to even imagine today, when there is an abundance of Italian food readily available worldwide. We take it for granted now.

Nonna, as all Italians are passionate and have a fiery side to them, we still remember how you would chase us with your slipper when we were being cheeky as children and trying to dip some bread into the pasta sauce to eat when you weren't looking. If we had been really naughty, it was a wooden spoon! Boy oh boy did you have an Italian temper, but we loved it!

Our Nonna is very much the matriarch and backbone of our *famiglia*. Nonna has sustained and strengthened the family through the culture of our people and our food. She is the strongest woman we have ever met. Nonna's food was a symbol of love and everyone adored it. She would cook and feed everyone and lived by the stove in her apron! The traditions she has taught us, we carry on today. *Mangia, mangia*, as our Nonna always says! *Nonna, ti vogliamo bene.* xx

Nonna Maria, center, holds her niece, with her family in the village in Italy where she was born. Her parents stand to her right and our beautiful Mamma to her left, being hugged by her cousins.

Contents

Acknowledgments 9

Introduction 11

Antipasti 21

Primi 61

Secondi 125

Dolci 163

Finale 205

Index 207

Acknowledgments

A huge Twintastico Twin kiss and thank-you to everyone at Pelican Publishing Company for believing in us and helping us make this book. We have wanted to write a cookbook for as long as we can remember, and now our dream has been turned into a reality. The biggest thank-you goes to everyone who has supported us—our family, our fans, and everyone who has believed in us since day one. You know who you are. *Grazie!*

Introduction

La Famiglia

"They say you can only make a first impression once. We make it twice!"

Ciao a tutti. Allow us to introduce ourselves. . . . We are the Alberti Twins, John and Tony, also known as the Italian Stallions and as Double Trouble.

With the huge success of our YouTube cooking channel, "Italian Cooking at Home with the Alberti Twins"; blog, www.TheAlbertiTwins.com, about food, fashion, and lifestyle; and cooking on TV around the world, we couldn't wait to share all of our Twintastico Italian family recipes with you in our debut cookbook.

Being born Italian and twins is like winning the lottery. We always say that being born Italian, we were born with our hearts on our sleeves and with a fire in our souls and mouths that we can't control.

Coming from an Italian family and growing up in England, we learned to cook by watching our parents and Nonna from an early age. We learned traditional Italian family recipes that were passed down through generations, and this is where our passion for food was born. We spent every summer on our family's farm in Italy, where we saw firsthand how food went from farm to table in homemade cheeses, bread, pasta, and sauces. They showed us how to prepare and cook some of the traditional Italian family recipes we share with you today.

Our family comes from the Garfagnana region of Tuscany, near Lucca. Italy is beautiful from top to toe, but for us, Tuscany is the most beautiful part. Once you go to Tuscany, you will never want to go anywhere else. Italy, the most magical place in the world, is where our hearts belong and is home for us. We love how Italy has never changed over the years, a testament to its strong culture and tradition. *La vita è bella* . . . life is beautiful, especially in Italy.

For us, Italy is the most beautiful country in the world. It has the best of everything—the best cars, the best fashion, the best food and wine, and most importantly the most beautiful people, culture, and tradition. You know the saying: "Italians do it better."

Raised the Italian way, we were brought up very traditionally and are very old-school Italians. Our parents raised us to be gentlemen. We have very strong morals and family values and have always been taught to have manners and be respectful. Being surrounded by strong, feisty, Italian women all our lives has made us appreciate, love, and respect all women.

We are so grateful for our parents and family, and we value every moment with them. We thank them for making us the gentlemen we are today and giving us a loving Italian family. The love of an Italian family is like no other. "Family first," we always say.

Family is everything! It will always be the most important thing in life. We come from a big Italian family. We are very passionate and proud of being Italian and our heritage. As we like to say, "Everybody wants to be Italian."

Being Italian, cooking is in our blood. So is romancing the women, but that's another story. Being Italian, for us it's all about family and food. We remember vividly sitting around the dining table as a family. We sat for hours and hours eating, drinking, laughing, and loving life. The Italian meal is meant to be an experience, full of atmosphere and lots of noise! This is the Italian way and how a meal should be spent, with family and great food and wine. This is something that was instilled in us from an early age and a tradition we will forever continue. Tradition is very important to Italians, and for tradition, you need time.

The kitchen and the dining table are the heart of the family home. A family that eats together stays together. An old Italian proverb, one our favorites, is *"a tavola con la famiglia, non si invecchia,"* which means "at the table with family, one does not age."

For us, family is sacred. A strong family provides mutual love, commitment, and honesty that allows you to grow up true to yourself. We want you to remember that the kitchen, with its environment and ritual, is where the whole family is united. The ritual of the table is a family's strongest bond. It is a way of life for us, and every week the whole family comes around for what we call "Spaghetti Sunday," for old-school Italian cooking. Everyone is Italian on Sunday.

Italians live to eat, not eat to live. We are always planning our next meal! Italian food and cooking should be enjoyed by the whole family, and the key is simplicity. Cooking should be done with passion and a love of food. It should be fun and involve the whole family, making it a tradition that can be passed down for generations to come. Let the ingredients do the talking. Use seasonal produce and cook with fresh ingredients, showcasing the best of what the land and sea have to offer. Let the seasons guide you when you cook and don't be a slave to recipes, even ours! We Italians like to add a bit of this and a bit of that when cooking; remember that Italians measure with their eyes. So let your heart and stomach guide you.

Our aim is to inspire and show you that you can look good and cook good and that food and fashion go hand in hand. We take pride in how we look and cook, and we treat the ingredients with respect. Remember that the most important ingredient in the kitchen will always be love. As we like to say, everything we cook is "irresistibly Italian."

We make it hot in the kitchen and want to show you that cooking is sexy. It should be done with style and passion, while you are looking your best. Italians are renowned for their style, passion, charm, and food. Remember that Italian food makes you beautiful . . . look at us!

To be a great cook, you have to be a great lover. You have to do it with passion or not at all, and Italians do it best. Remember when cooking to have fun and cook with passion and love. Italian food is the most romantic in the world. It is the food of love. *Amore!*

Italians know how to do things in style. We always take our time and never rush anything, whether that be inside the kitchen or out. An Italian meal can go on for hours. We have a saying in Italy—*"dolce far niente"*—which means "the sweetness of doing nothing," and we Italians are the masters of it.

Italian food speaks to the soul, and it is loved around the world for its simplicity and romance. We want to show you that Italian food can be eaten every day and you can still look amazing. The benefits of the Mediterranean diet, which is why Italians live such long, beautiful, healthy, and fruitful lives, are evident for all to see.

We want to show you that you do not have to be a professionally trained chef to cook great food at home for you and your family. Cooking is an act of love, a gift, a way of sharing, and should be enjoyed and bring the whole family together. We want families to cook together again, eat together at the table, and pass on this tradition and love of food.

To all the ladies reading this, if you ever meet us, you will definitely be greeted with two kisses from each of us. As we always say, "Kiss a lady on both cheeks when you greet her." That's what she has two cheeks for, a kiss for each one. This is something we have always been taught and is very Italian.

Throughout the cookbook, we will be sharing with you our homemade traditional Italian family recipes passed down through generations, for you to cook and enjoy at home with all your family. We want to take you on a journey through a traditional Italian meal from start to finish. We love to be inventive in the kitchen, so you will find lots of Italian Twintastico Twists on classic recipes along the way, done Alberti Style. *Forza Italia!*

Grazie to you all for choosing our cookbook. We hope to inspire you to cook Italian at home and love food the way it should be loved, Italian style. Enjoy and *buon appetito!*

- Twitter—@Tony_Alberti, @John_Alberti
- Instagram—The_Alberti_Twins
- Blog—www.TheAlbertiTwins.com
- YouTube cooking channel—"Italian Cooking at Home with the Alberti Twins"

Who's who?

Alberti Day, June 2, 1635, New York City

We always knew there would be a day named after us. . . .

We love New York and have always felt a strong connection to the city. We visit regularly to cook on TV, see friends, and find new, interesting, unique places to eat and drink. We always go to Battery Park in Lower Manhattan, where there is our very own Alberti Day monument. We are proud to be Albertis, and here is how Alberti Day came about.

His name was Pietro Cesare Alberti (later changed to Peter Caesar Alberti) from Venice, and he was the first Italian settler in New Amsterdam.

The year was 1635 and the setting was Dutch New Amsterdam (the future NYC)—a fledgling town suffering from government mismanagement, lack of support from its primary financial backer the Dutch West India Company, and the constant threat of takeover from the other European powers vying for colonial supremacy. Into this uncertainty stepped Pietro, the son of Andrea Alberti, secretary of the treasury of Venice, and Lady Veronica, a descendant of the great Medici family.

Pietro was a sailor by trade and his career began in the employ of the Dutch, as they were trading partners with the Venetian Republic. He served as an officer and advisor to David Pietersen, the captain of the Dutch ship King David, which was scheduled to explore the New World. One such trip required the King David to sail into the New Amsterdam harbor to make ship repairs. After a dispute with Captain Pietersen, Alberti (who was in his mid-twenties) decided to stay ashore on Manhattan Island and make a new life for himself. While he was the only Italian in the city of New Amsterdam, he adapted very well. He became a successful tobacco farmer in what is today land stretching from the Brooklyn Navy Yard to Fort Greene, in addition to owning a house and land on Broad Street in modern-day Manhattan. Alberti married into the Dutch aristocracy but was later killed on his farm, along with his wife, Judith Manje, in a raid by Native Americans in 1655. He had seven children who married into such early influential New York families as the Wyckoffs, Remsens, Motts, and Nostrands—names that to this day dot the streetscape of New York.

The monument was in Bowling Green park before being moved to the perimeter of Battery Park between Greenwich and Washington streets.

Make sure to visit the spot where the first Italian-American, our ancestor Pietro Cesare Alberti, left his mark and opened the door for future immigrant generations to come. One small step for Pietro Cesare Alberti became a giant leap for Italian-Americans.

This photo was taken in 2014, before the monument was moved.

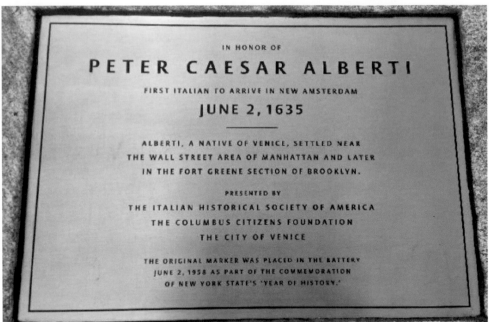

The monument at its new location, 2015.

The Alberti family circa 1900.

Conversion Chart

Liquid Measures

Fluid Ounces	U.S.	Imperial	Milliliters
	1 teaspoon	1 teaspoon	5
1/3	2 teaspoons	1 dessertspoon	10
1/2	1 tablespoon	1 tablespoon	14
1	2 tablespoons	2 tablespoons	28
2	1/4 cup	4 tablespoons	56
4	1/2 cup		120
5		1/4 pint	140
6	3/4 cup		170
8	1 cup		240
9			250 or 1/4 liter
10	1 1/4 cups	1/2 pint	280
12	1 1/2 cups		340
15		3/4 pint	420
16	2 cups		450
18	2 1/4 cups		500 or 1/2 liter
20	2 1/2 cups	1 pint	560
24	3 cups		675
25		1 1/4 pints	700
27	3 1/2 cups		750
30	3 3/4 cups	1 1/2 pints	840
32	4 cups		900
35		1 3/4 pints	980
36	4 1/2 cups		1000 or 1 liter
40	5 cups	2 pints	1120

Solid Measures

U.S. and Imperial Measures		Metric Measures	
Ounces	Pounds	Grams	Kilos
1		28	
2		56	
3 1/2		100	
4	1/4	112	
5		140	
6		168	
8	1/2	225	
9		250	1/4
12	3/4	340	
16	1	450	
18		500	1/2
20	1 1/4	560	
24	1 1/2	675	
27		750	3/4
28	1 3/4	780	
32	2	900	
36	2 1/4	1000	1
40	2 1/2	1100	
48	3	1350	
54		1500	1 1/2

Oven Temperature Equivalents

Fahrenheit	Celsius	Gas Mark	Description
225	110	¼	Cool
250	130	½	
275	140	1	Very Slow
300	150	2	
325	170	3	Slow
350	180	4	Moderate
375	190	5	
400	200	6	Moderately Hot
425	220	7	Fairly Hot
450	230	8	Hot
475	240	9	Very Hot
500	250	10	Extremely Hot

Twintastico

Italian Cooking at Home with the Alberti Twins

Antipasti

This is the meal before the meal and our favorite. Basically, it is an appetizer and literally means "before the meal." This course traditionally precedes the pasta. Antipasti offers a wide variety of cured meats such as prosciutto and salami, bruschetta (toasted bread with tomatoes and other toppings), a selection of breads, pickled or fried vegetables, marinated mushrooms, and olives. These are typically served as small dishes at the table. This course is usually accompanied with an *aperitivo*, which is a predinner drink designed to open the palate. A typical drink for an aperitivo is Prosecco, Campari soda, or—our favorite—an Aperol spritz.

First we eat, then we do everything else.

Bella Broad Bean Dip

This is our go-to dip and a family favorite. It is refreshing, bright, tangy, and perfect for dipping and spreading. Broad beans (fava beans) and pecorino go together beautifully. Use this as a dip, or spread on crostini.

2 cups broad (fava) beans or edamame beans
Juice of ½ lemon
1 garlic clove
1 handful fresh mint leaves
¾ cup grated pecorino Romano
Drizzle of extra-virgin olive oil
Salt and pepper

Bring a saucepan of water to a boil and cook the beans for 5 minutes. Drain and, when cool enough to handle, remove the skins.

Put the beans in a food processor with the lemon juice, garlic, mint, pecorino, and extra-virgin olive oil. Season with salt and pepper and blend to form a coarse paste. Serve as a dip or on crostini.

Serves 4-6

Blessed Basil Pesto

"Pesto is besto!"

Here is our traditional basil pesto. For us, the smell of basil reminds us of home in Italy. It is one of the most beautiful smells in the world. Pesto is easy and quick to make and tastes incredible. It can be used with all types of pasta, on bread, and for dipping.

2 garlic cloves
Pinch of salt
⅓ cup fresh basil leaves
⅓ cup pine nuts
1 cup grated Parmigiano Reggiano
Drizzle of extra-virgin olive oil

If you're making this in a mortar and pestle, put in the garlic and salt and pound to a rough paste. Add the basil leaves and pound them down. Then add the pine nuts and Parmigiano Reggiano. Continue pounding the mixture until you get a paste. Gradually drizzle in the olive oil, mixing it in until combined.

If you're making this in a food processor or blender, pulse the garlic, salt, and pine nuts together a few times to a rough paste. Add the basil leaves and pulse again. Continue pulsing until you get a paste. Gradually add the oil, pulsing as you go until just combined. Then finally add the Parmigiano Reggiano and pulse a few times until combined.

Serves 4-6

Mamma Mia Marinara Sauce

"Everyone is Italian on Sunday."

Every Italian family has their own sauce that they swear by. This is our Mamma's sauce that we grew up on and why we look so good today! It's our go-to recipe when we want something very tasty and easy. It is a favorite in our house to add to spaghetti for our "Spaghetti Sunday." Making pasta sauce is really easy and you can prepare it in no time at all. This sauce is so versatile it can be used with pasta, poultry, meat, and fish and for dipping. The secret ingredient is the sage. It gives an earthy, warming flavor and adds depth to the sauce.

5 garlic cloves, finely chopped
Extra-virgin olive oil
4 cups tomato puree
2 tbsp. tomato paste
10 fresh basil leaves, finely chopped
6 sage leaves, finely chopped
Salt and pepper

In a large skillet over medium heat, cook the garlic in the oil until the garlic sizzles and turns golden. Then add the tomato puree, tomato paste, basil, and sage. Season with salt and pepper and stir. Reduce heat and simmer for about 45 minutes until the sauce reduces and thickens.

Serves 4-6

Italia's Creamy Cannellini Dip

"You say hummus; we say cannellini."

It's dippable, lickable, and spreadable! It's cheap to make, healthy, quick, and packed with flavor—the perfect dip. Here is our Italian twist on the classic hummus. . . . Italians do it better!

4 cups cannellini beans
1 garlic clove
Juice of ½ lemon
Salt and pepper
Drizzle of extra-virgin olive oil

Drain and rinse the cannellini beans and add to a blender. Add the garlic and lemon juice, season with salt and pepper, and blend. Once at a smooth consistency, add extra-virgin olive oil and blend again to get a silky texture. Tip into a serving bowl and serve.

This dip is very versatile. Sprinkle red pepper flakes on top if you want a little extra kick. You can also add a roasted red pepper to the mix and blend, if you want a different color and flavor.

Serves 4-6

Addictive Anchovy and Sage Fritti

Simple, quick, crispy, and full of flavor—this is a well-balanced snack that everyone will enjoy, even the non-anchovy lovers. We promise!

1½ cups all-purpose flour
1 egg, lightly beaten
Salt
½ cup sparkling water
Olive oil or vegetable oil for frying
20 anchovy fillets
40 large sage leaves
Pepper
Lemon wedges

For batter, in a large bowl, combine flour, egg, and a large pinch of salt. Add sparkling water and mix until a smooth, thin batter forms.

Heat the oil over medium heat in a deep, heavy-bottomed skillet to 350F. Sandwich 1 anchovy between 2 large sage leaves and dip into the batter, coating well. Repeat with remaining anchovies and sage leaves. Gently place the sage leaves into the hot oil and fry until golden and crispy.

Transfer to a plate lined with a paper towel. Sprinkle with salt and pepper and serve with a squeeze of lemon.

Makes 20

Zucchini Fritti

We love zucchini fritti and always order them when in restaurants, so making these at home is even better. Zucchini are probably the most used vegetable in Italy. Though the zucchini may be humble, it produces wonderful results. It can be eaten raw, fried in slices, baked or grilled whole, stuffed, or used in lasagna. It' quick, easy, and delicious.

6 zucchini
Olive oil or vegetable oil for frying
1½ cups all-purpose flour
½ cup sparkling water
1 egg, lightly beaten
Salt and pepper
Lemon wedges

Trim the ends off the zucchini and cut the zucchini in half lengthwise. Cut out the white center and seeds, if any (this part is too watery for frying), and cut the remainder lengthwise into batons (sticks). Cut these in half crosswise, so that you are left with matchsticks about 2 inches long.

Heat the oil over medium heat in a large, deep skillet to 350F.

Meanwhile, mix the flour, water, and egg to make a light batter. Season with salt and pepper. Dip a handful of the zucchini matchsticks into the batter.

Test a drop of batter in the oil—it should sizzle and turn brown in a few seconds. When the oil is hot, plunge the handful of battered zucchini matchsticks into it. Deep fry them in batches, separating them with a spoon, until they are crisp and golden, about 4-5 minutes.

Drain well on a paper towel. Sprinkle with salt and pepper and serve with a squeeze of lemon.

Serves 4-6

Polenta Fries with Aioli Dip

Polenta is so versatile and very underused, in our opinion. We love to make polenta fries and prefer them to regular fries. They have great texture and taste amazing. These are served with a quick aioli dip.

POLENTA FRIES

4 cups water
1 cup polenta
Salt and pepper
½ cup grated Parmigiano Reggiano, plus extra for serving
½ stick butter
2 tbsp. fresh rosemary, finely chopped
Extra-virgin olive oil

AIOLI DIP

¾ cup mayonnaise
2 garlic cloves, finely chopped
Drizzle of extra-virgin olive oil
Squeeze of lemon juice
Salt and pepper

Bring the water to a boil and slowly whisk in the polenta, stirring constantly. Season with salt and pepper. After a few minutes, once thickened, add ½ cup Parmigiano Reggiano, the butter, and the rosemary. Combine until smooth.

Pour into a greased and lined 8x8-inch baking pan, and pop into the fridge to chill and firm up, about 2 hours.

Preheat oven to 425F. Cut the chilled polenta into chunky fries and brush with olive oil. Arrange on a greased baking sheet in a single layer and bake for 30 minutes, or until crisp and golden.

To make the aioli dip, in a small bowl, mix the mayonnaise, garlic, olive oil, and lemon juice. Season to taste with salt and pepper. This is very quick and easy and packs a punch.

Season the polenta fries again. Serve with extra Parmigiano Reggiano grated on top and the aioli dip on the side.

Serves 4-6

Pretty Polenta Crostini

Polenta crostini are made by spreading cooked polenta into a thin layer, allowing it to cool, and then cutting it into squares. These cute little snacks are full of flavor and texture. Crostini can be baked, broiled, grilled, or deep fried. Use polenta crostini as a base for appetizers, part of the antipasti.

½ cup dried or fresh porcini mushrooms
4 cups water
1 cup polenta
1 cup grated Parmigiano Reggiano
1½ sticks butter, divided
Salt and pepper
Extra-virgin olive oil
Ragu sauce, optional (see index for Twintastico Tagliatelle al Ragu)

If using dried porcini mushrooms, soak in warm water for about 30 minutes to soften. Remove the mushrooms from the liquid (you can keep the porcini mushroom stock to add to the polenta if you wish or use when making risotto). Chop the mushrooms coarsely and set aside.

Over high heat, in a heavy saucepan, bring the water to a boil. Add the polenta gradually, whisking constantly. Reduce the heat to low and cook, stirring occasionally. Add the Parmigiano Reggiano, 1 stick butter, salt, and pepper, and stir to combine.

Pour the polenta into a greased 9x9-inch baking pan, spreading so that it is about ⅓ inch thick. Cover and chill in the refrigerator overnight.

Preheat oven to 400F.

Cut the polenta into equal bitesize squares and brush each piece with olive oil. Place on a baking sheet and cook in the oven for 30 minutes until golden and crisp.

In the meantime, add a drizzle of extra-virgin olive oil to a skillet. Add ½ stick butter. Add the coarsely chopped porcini mushrooms and fry for about 5 minutes. Place polenta crostini on a plate and top with the porcini mushrooms or ragu meat sauce.

Serves 4-6

Fantastico Calamari Fritti

If you know us, you know we love calamari. We could eat it all day! This simple, quick dish brings back memories of our childhood at the seaside in Italy, sitting with our family in the sun and enjoying fresh, crispy calamari.

1 lb. 2 oz. squid
Vegetable oil for frying
2 cups all-purpose flour
Salt and pepper
Lemon wedges

Slice the calamari into ¼-inch-thick rings. Pour enough oil into a heavy, large saucepan to reach the depth of about 3 inches. Heat over medium heat to 350F.

In a large bowl, mix the flour with salt and pepper. Then toss the calamari in the flour and shake off any excess. Deep fry in batches for about 1 minute until crispy and golden. Remove with a slotted spoon and drain any excess oil on paper towels.

Season again with salt. Add a squeeze of lemon and serve with our Mamma Mia Marinara Sauce or Aioli Dip, if desired.

Serves 4-6

4 cups vegetable stock
1 stick butter
Extra-virgin olive oil
6 shallots, finely chopped
2¼ cups Arborio rice
1 cup dry Italian white wine
1 cup grated Parmigiano Reggiano
Salt and pepper
1 cup cubed mozzarella
2 cups all-purpose flour
4 eggs, lightly beaten
2 cups dried breadcrumbs
Vegetable oil for frying

Alberti's Arancini Golden Italian Balls

"Everyone loves our Golden Italian Balls!"

When you have leftover risotto, this is a great recipe to make. Crispy on the outside and soft and gooey on the inside, these big, juicy Golden Italian Balls are perfect for snacking on.

In a large saucepan over high heat, bring the vegetable stock to a simmer. Reduce the heat to low and keep the stock hot.

In a large, deep, heavy saucepan over medium heat, melt the butter and drizzle in a little extra-virgin olive oil. Add the shallots and cook, stirring frequently, for about 3 minutes. Add the rice and stir to coat with the butter. Add the wine and simmer until most of the liquid has evaporated, about 2 minutes.

Add a ladle of the vegetable stock and stir until almost completely absorbed, about 2 minutes. Continue cooking the rice, adding the stock a ladle at a time, stirring constantly and allowing each addition of the stock to absorb before adding the next. Cook until the rice is tender but still firm to the bite and the mixture is creamy, about 20 minutes. Remove the pan from the heat and add Parmigiano Reggiano, salt, and pepper. Mix well and leave to cool.

Once the risotto is cooled (it doesn't matter if it is still a little warm, as long as it has stiffened up a bit and is cool enough to handle), with damp hands, roll into balls the size of golf balls. Push a piece of mozzarella into the middle of each ball, making sure that the cheese is completely enclosed. Leave to set in the fridge for at least 30 minutes or overnight.

Lay out 3 plates or shallow bowls. Put the flour (seasoned with a pinch of salt and pepper) in one, the beaten eggs in another, and the breadcrumbs in the final one.

In a large, heavy-bottomed saucepan, pour in enough oil to fill the pan about ⅓ of the way, or use a deep-fat fryer. Heat over medium heat to 350F. (If you don't have a deep-frying thermometer, test with a cube of bread, which will brown in about 2 minutes when the oil is 350F.)

Dip an arancini ball into the flour, then into the eggs, and finish by coating completely in the breadcrumbs. Repeat with the remaining balls.

In batches, fry the rice balls, turning occasionally, until golden, about 4-5 minutes. Drain on paper towels and serve.

Serves 4-6

Tuscan Crostini with Chicken Liver Pâté

These rustic crostini are perfect as part of the antipasti or little snacks for family and friends and will make you go back for more and more. Rich and bold in flavor, they will definitely leave you satisfied . . . just like us!

1 large red onion, finely chopped
Extra-virgin olive oil
½ stick butter
2 garlic cloves, finely chopped
10 anchovy fillets, drained of oil
15 capers
1 lb. chicken livers
5 sage leaves, finely chopped
1 cup Vin Santo or marsala wine
Salt and pepper
1 baguette or ciabatta

In a large, deep skillet, cook the onion in the olive oil and butter until soft and translucent. Add the garlic, anchovies, and capers, and continue to sauté until the anchovies melt down. Add the chicken livers and sauté until browned on all sides.

Add the sage leaves and Vin Santo or marsala wine. Cook on low, uncovered, and leave to simmer for about 30 minutes. Season with salt and pepper.

Transfer the hot mixture to a food processor or blender and blend until mostly smooth (or completely smooth, if you prefer that consistency). Cut the bread into thin, ½-inch slices and lightly brush the bread with olive oil. Bake at 350F until crisp and golden, about 15 minutes.

Place heaped tablespoons of the pâté onto the bread and serve.

Serves 4-6

Fabulicious Farro

This dish is packed with color and flavor and excites the eyes and taste buds. We love farro, a nutty ancient grain, and this recipe is very easy and quick to make. It will definitely keep your family and friends happy. It is perfect as antipasti or as part of the main meal. If you can't get hold of farro, barley is a great alternative.

2 cups uncooked farro
4 cups salted water
Salt and pepper
Extra-virgin olive oil
Drizzle of white wine vinegar
1 red pepper, cubed
1 green pepper, cubed
1 yellow pepper, cubed
2 carrots, peeled and cubed
1 red onion, finely chopped
¼ cup chopped black olives
10 fresh basil leaves, finely chopped

Bring the farro to a boil in the water, then simmer for 25 minutes until tender. It should still be chewy and nutty when cooked. Drain well, season with salt and pepper, and drizzle with extra-virgin olive oil and white wine vinegar. Mix well and leave to cool.

Once cooled, add the peppers, carrots, red onion, black olives, and basil. Drizzle with some more extra-virgin olive oil. Mix well and season with salt and pepper if needed. Then place in the refrigerator for a few hours until ready to eat. This dish is best served cold.

This recipe is very versatile and you can add lots of different ingredients, such as cooked vegetables (zucchini, eggplant, mushrooms), sliced fennel, artichokes, pickles, and much more!

Serves 4-6

Figtastic Summer Salad

"A salad should be well dressed . . . just like an Italian."

This is the most amazing, delicious salad you will ever set your eyes on or eat. With its gorgeous colors, it tastes as good as it looks! Radicchio has a bitter flavor and contrasts well with milder leaves such as arugula. Try chicory as an alternative. The bitterness of the radicchio and sharpness of the gorgonzola piccante contrast so well with the sweetness of the figs and balsamic vinegar. They work perfectly together. Fresh, quick, and packed full of flavor, this salad is perfect for the summer. It really is summer on a plate.

1 large head radicchio or chicory
1 red onion, thinly sliced
10 fresh basil leaves
½ cup arugula leaves
½ cup halved cherry tomatoes
Extra-virgin olive oil
Balsamic vinegar
Salt and pepper
5 fresh figs, quartered
½ cup crumbled gorgonzola piccante cheese
½ cup walnut halves

Cut the radicchio and add to a large bowl. Then add the sliced red onion, basil, arugula, and halved cherry tomatoes. Drizzle with extra-virgin olive oil and balsamic vinegar and season with salt and pepper. Adding salt to the cherry tomatoes will really bring out their full flavor. Give these ingredients a good mix with your hands and make sure all are coated and completely combined.

Pour the mixture onto a large platter and spread out evenly. This is already looking seductively summery.

Top with the figs, crumble on the gorgonzola piccante, and sprinkle on the walnuts. To finish this stunning salad, drizzle a little extra-virgin olive oil over it.

Serves 4-6

Caesar Salad

The classic Caesar salad is known around the world. Here is our special recipe that is packed with flavor, with a Twintastico Twist!

DRESSING

3 garlic cloves, minced
4 anchovy fillets, finely chopped
¼ cup fresh lemon juice
1 tbsp. Dijon mustard
2 large egg yolks
1 tsp. Worcestershire sauce
½ cup extra-virgin olive oil
½ cup grated Parmigiano Reggiano
Salt and freshly ground pepper

POLENTA CROUTONS

4 cups water
1 tsp. salt
1 cup polenta
2 tbsp. unsalted butter
1 cup grated Parmigiano Reggiano
Extra-virgin olive oil
Vegetable oil for frying

SALAD

2 large heads romaine lettuce, leaves separated
Grated Parmigiano Reggiano

To make the dressing, in a large bowl, mash garlic and anchovies together into a paste. Add the lemon juice and mustard, and mix well. Now add the yolks and Worcestershire sauce, and mix together. Gradually blend in the oil. Whisk in the Parmigiano Reggiano, and season with salt and pepper.

To make the polenta croutons, in a large saucepan, bring the water to a boil and season with salt. Gradually whisk in the polenta. Reduce the heat to low and cook until the mixture thickens, stirring often, about 10 minutes. Turn off the heat. Add the butter and Parmigiano Reggiano and stir until melted.

Spread a little extra-virgin olive oil over a small baking sheet. Transfer the polenta to the baking sheet, spreading evenly to form an 8x5-inch rectangle that is ¾ inch thick. Cover and refrigerate until cold and firm, about 2 hours.

Cut the polenta into ¾-inch cubes. In a large skillet, add about ½ inch vegetable oil. Heat the oil over high heat. Working in batches of 10, carefully add the polenta cubes to the oil 1 at a time and fry until golden brown, stirring to keep the cubes separate, about 5 minutes. Using a slotted spoon, transfer the polenta croutons to a paper-towel-lined plate to drain any excess oil.

To make the salad, add the lettuce leaves to the dressing and toss well to combine. Scatter the warm polenta croutons over the salad, sprinkle extra Parmigiano Reggiano on top, and serve immediately.

Serves 4-6

Piccoli Cuscini

We like to call pasta fritta "little cushions"—piccoli cuscini—because they puff up when fried. They are always on the menu in Tuscany as part of the antipasti. Antipasti is our favorite course and is so irresistible that we are often nearly too full when the primi and secondi courses arrive! You could even stuff the piccoli cuscini with cured meats and/or cheeses.

2 cups all-purpose flour
2¼ tsp. fast-acting dry yeast
1 tsp. sugar
1 tbsp. salt
1 cup water
Extra-virgin olive oil
Olive oil or vegetable oil for frying

Add the flour, yeast, sugar, and salt to a large bowl and mix well. Then add the water and combine. Transfer to a floured work surface and knead for about 5 minutes until smooth.

Lightly oil a large bowl, shape the dough into a ball, and coat with the olive oil that is in the bowl. Cover bowl with plastic wrap. Let dough stand for about 2 hours until doubled in size.

Once doubled in size, cut the dough in half. Using a rolling pin on a floured work surface, roll 1 piece out into a sheet about ¼ inch thick. Using a pasta cutter or pastry wheel, cut into small squares, rectangles, or diamonds, about 2 inches wide. Repeat with remaining dough.

Heat oil in a large, deep skillet over medium heat to 350F. Start to fry, adding a few at a time and turning as they start to turn golden. Remove with a slotted spoon and drain in a bowl on paper towels. Season each batch with plenty of salt and serve.

Makes about 40

Crunchy Crostini

Crostini means "little crusts" in Italian. They are the perfect snack and very delicious, especially when served with honey, cheese, or dip. Here is our family recipe. It is so easy to make and great fun to get the children involved.

2 cups all-purpose flour
1 tsp. salt
1 cup water
Drizzle of extra-virgin olive oil
Coarse sea salt
Pepper
Rosemary, finely chopped

In a large mixing bowl, add the flour, 1 tsp. salt, water, and extra-virgin olive oil. Mix together well to create a dough. Then knead the dough on a lightly floured surface for 1 minute.

Divide the dough in half. Using a rolling pin, roll out 1 piece and transfer to ungreased baking sheet. Roll it very thin, as it will rise in the oven. Repeat with the second piece.

With a fork, make little holes all over the surface of the dough. Sprinkle coarse sea salt, pepper, and rosemary on top of each sheet. Using a rotary pizza cutter, cut the dough into small squares. It doesn't matter if they aren't perfect. They're not supposed to be—they are a rustic snack.

Preheat oven to 350F. Bake crostini for 15-20 minutes until golden. Keep an eye on them, as some may cook faster than others, depending on their size.

Let cool, then enjoy these beautiful, simple snacks.

Makes about 30

Holy Focaccia

This is one of our favorite types of bread to make and eat. Easy to make and extremely delicious. Perfect for dipping into balsamic vinegar and extra-virgin olive oil and for mopping up our Italian sauce.

2 cups all-purpose or bread flour
½ cup extra-virgin olive oil
1 tsp. superfine sugar
2¼ tsp. fast-acting dry yeast
1 cup water
1 tbsp. salt
2 tbsp. fresh rosemary, finely chopped
Coarse sea salt

In a large mixing bowl, add the flour and then the olive oil, sugar, yeast, water, and salt. Using a sturdy wooden spoon, mix together well.

Turn the dough out onto a floured work surface and knead, adding more flour if needed, for about 10 minutes. It should be smooth and springy to the touch.

Lightly oil a large bowl, shape the dough into a ball, and coat with the olive oil that is in the bowl. Cover bowl with a damp towel and let dough stand for about 2 hours until doubled in size. Lightly oil a 13x9-inch baking sheet, and using your hands, stretch out the dough to fill the sheet. Cover and let stand for another 30 minutes.

Preheat oven to 425F.

Now, use your fingers—or ladies, if you've just had a manicure and don't want to ruin your nails, use the handle of a wooden spoon—to make those beautiful dimples on top of the dough. Drizzle the top with extra-virgin olive oil and sprinkle the whole surface with chopped rosemary and sea salt. If you prefer, rather than sprinkling on chopped rosemary, you can stuff rosemary sprigs into the dimples.

Bake for 20-25 minutes until golden brown. Then cut into squares and enjoy this beautiful focaccia with the whole family, the way it's supposed to be.

Makes 1 large loaf

Pane di Patate

"Let's break bread."

Pane di patate *means "potato bread" in Italian. In the Garfagnana region of Tuscany, where our family is from, the local potato bread is called Garfagnino. To Italians, tradition is everything. The combination of flour and potato makes the bread softer and provides an unforgettable, full flavor.*

2 potatoes
2 cups all-purpose flour
2¼ tsp. fast-acting dry yeast
1 tbsp. salt
Extra-virgin olive oil

Peel and boil the potatoes in salted water until tender. Drain, reserving 2 cups of the cooking water. Let the water and potatoes cool, then thoroughly mash the potatoes until smooth.

In a large bowl, combine the flour, yeast, potatoes, and salt. Stir in enough of the reserved water to form a dough.

Turn the dough out onto a lightly floured surface and knead for about 5 minutes or until it has a soft, satiny, elastic texture. If the dough seems too wet, add more flour sparingly. Place the dough in an oiled bowl, cover with plastic wrap, and let rise until doubled in size.

Line a baking sheet with parchment paper. Gently punch down the dough and shape into a round, somewhat flat loaf. Place on the prepared baking sheet, cover with a kitchen towel, and let rise again for 30-60 minutes.

Preheat oven to 400F.

Score the top of the bread. Bake for 30-40 minutes until golden brown and the bottom of the loaf sounds hollow when tapped. Reduce the oven temperature slightly if the loaf is browning too quickly. Transfer the loaf to a wire rack and let cool.

Makes 1 large loaf

Pane Toscano

"Patience is a virtue."

Italians love bread, and this is a classic. This typical Tuscan bread, which contains no salt, is always on the table to accompany a meal. It is perfect for mopping up pasta sauce and soups, dipping in olive oil, and topping with meats and cheeses. We remember as kids going into restaurants in Italy with our family and waiting eagerly to get our hands on the bread, to dip in olive oil and the sauce. This recipe requires effort and patience but is so worth it! The chewy yet crunchy crust and light yeastiness make Tuscan bread unique and unforgettable.

STARTER

2¼ tsp. fast-acting dry yeast
½ cup water
1 cup all-purpose or bread flour

DOUGH

2 cups all-purpose or bread flour
1 cup water

To make the starter, sprinkle the yeast into the water in a bowl. Stir and let stand for 5 minutes to dissolve the yeast. Add the flour and mix to form a thick paste. Cover with plastic wrap and let stand at room temperature for at least 12 hours to ferment.

To make the dough, put the flour into a large bowl, make a well in the center, and add the starter to the well. Add the water and mix well to form a wet dough.

Cover with plastic wrap and let rise for about 1 hour until doubled in size. Turn the dough out onto a well-floured work surface and knead for about 10 minutes. Add flour to the dough if needed, but it should still be moist.

Shape the dough into an oval loaf, and place onto an oiled baking sheet. Cover with a kitchen towel and proof for about 30 minutes.

Preheat oven to 400 F.

Using a sieve, lightly dust flour over the loaf, and then score the top in the shape of an X. Bake for 45-50 minutes until golden on top and the bottom of the loaf sounds hollow when tapped. Transfer the loaf to a wire rack and let cool.

Makes 1 large loaf

Primi

Primi, or "first dishes," follow the antipasti and usually include pasta, risotto, or soup. Pasta, of course, comes in an endless variety of shapes, sizes, textures, and sauces. Here are some of our favorite primi, along with Italian Twintastico Twists on some classic recipes.

Everything you see, we owe to spaghetti.

Italian Eggs Benedict

"How do you like your eggs in the morning? We like ours with a kiss."

Eggs Benedict is a favorite dish around the world. Here is our Italian Twintastico Twist on the classic recipe. The pancetta (Italian cured pork belly) adds texture and a nice saltiness to the dish, and the Parmigiano Reggiano takes the hollandaise sauce to the next level, giving it a rich, creamier taste. This is an eggcellent recipe if we do say so ourselves!

⅔ cup pancetta cubes
Extra-virgin olive oil
⅔ cup butter
3 egg yolks
1 tbsp. Dijon mustard
¼ cup grated Parmigiano Reggiano
3 tbsp. white wine vinegar
Salt and pepper
1 ciabatta bread
2 large eggs
Handful of coarsely chopped chives

Fry the pancetta in a skillet with a little extra-virgin olive oil until crispy, about 5 minutes. Set aside.

To make the hollandaise sauce, melt the butter in a small pan. Place the egg yolks in the top of a double boiler over a saucepan of gently simmering water. Whisk the yolks together with the mustard. Whisking constantly, very slowly (otherwise it will break) pour in the melted butter. Add the Parmigiano Reggiano and whisk into the egg mixture until well combined, adding a splash of water to loosen, if needed. Whisk in the white wine vinegar and season to perfection. Turn off the heat and keep warm over the pan of water, stirring occasionally and loosening with an extra splash of water if needed.

Cut the ciabatta in half lengthwise. Drizzle the cut sides with extra-virgin olive oil, and place cut side down on a very hot griddle to brown.

To poach the eggs, boil water in a pan and add a splash of vinegar. Crack 1 egg into a little bowl. Add the egg gently to the pan. Repeat with the other egg. Leave in the pan for 3 minutes.

Place the poached eggs on the cut sides of the ciabatta. Add the sauce generously over the eggs, then sprinkle the pancetta and chopped chives on top to finish.

Serves 2

La Frittata

The Italian omelet is the Breakfast of Champions. As Italians, our usual breakfast is a cappuccino and an Italian pastry, but when you need something a little more, this is the perfect choice. It is filling, packed with flavor, and sure to set you up for the beautiful day ahead.

Extra-virgin olive oil
½ zucchini, thinly sliced
1 large onion, thinly sliced
1 red bell pepper, finely chopped
¼ cup thinly sliced porcini mushrooms
2 garlic cloves, finely chopped
8 eggs
Salt and pepper
Bunch of fresh basil leaves
Bunch of fresh spinach
½ cup grated Parmigiano Reggiano
¾ cup shredded mozzarella
¼ cup coarsely chopped sundried tomatoes

In a large, deep, nonstick skillet over medium heat, add extra-virgin olive oil. Add the zucchini, onions, peppers, and mushrooms, and cook for about 5 minutes. Add the garlic and cook for 1 more minute.

In a large bowl, beat eggs with salt and pepper until light in color and well mixed. Pour eggs into the hot skillet. Sprinkle on the basil and spinach, and cook for 3-4 minutes or until mixture is almost set.

Sprinkle Parmigiano Reggiano, mozzarella, and sundried tomatoes over half of omelet. Season with salt and pepper. Run a spatula lightly under the other half to make sure it's not stuck, then gently fold the egg mixture over the filling. Let cook for 1-2 more minutes to allow the cheese to melt, then slide the omelet out of the skillet onto a plate.

Serves 2

Tasty Tomato and Basil Soup

Making your own tasty tomato soup is so easy! Our soup will keep you warm and snug on those cold winter nights, just like Italians do. Add a little red pepper flakes if you want a bit of a kick.

Extra-virgin olive oil
2½ lb. vine-ripened tomatoes, whole
2 tbsp. tomato paste
3 garlic cloves, finely chopped
Handful of fresh basil leaves
1½ cups vegetable stock
Salt and pepper
1½ cups heavy cream
Red pepper flakes, optional

Heat a large, heavy-bottomed saucepan over medium-high heat. Add extra virgin olive oil, then add the tomatoes and cook for 5 minutes, or until they have started to break down.

Add the tomato paste, garlic, and basil, and cook for 1 minute. Pour in the vegetable stock, and bring the mixture to a boil. Reduce the heat and simmer the mixture for 10 minutes.

Transfer the mixture to a food processor and blend to a purée. Return the blended soup to the pan and season. Pour in the cream and return the mixture to a simmer. Continue to simmer for 1-2 minutes.

To serve, ladle the soup into 4 serving bowls. Drizzle a swirl of heavy cream into each bowl, red pepper flakes if desired, then a swirl of extra-virgin olive oil. Garnish with a few basil leaves and serve.

Serves 4

Nonna's Tortellini en Brodo

Our Nonna Maria is our biggest inspiration in and out of the kitchen, and this is one of her favorites. **Brodo** *means "broth" in Italian. This soup will make you live forever . . . or so our Nonna says. We love you, Nonna!*

Extra-virgin olive oil
1 large carrot, peeled and thinly sliced
2 celery stalks, finely chopped
1 onion, finely chopped
Salt and pepper
2½ cups chicken or vegetable stock
1 lb. tortellini
Small bunch of flat-leaf parsley, finely chopped
Grated Parmigiano Reggiano

In a large pot over medium heat, add the olive oil. Add the carrots, celery, and onions, and season with salt and pepper. Cook for about 5 minutes.

Add stock and reduce heat. Simmer for about 30 minutes.

Bring the soup to a boil. Add the tortellini, and cook for about 3 minutes, or until they rise to the surface. Season with salt and pepper, and ladle soup into bowls. Sprinkle the chopped parsley on top, and serve with grated Parmigiano Reggiano.

Serves 4

Twinning Tuscan Vegetable Soup

"Keep warm in winter. . . . Eat Italian."

For the cold winter months, this is exactly what you need to keep warm. Everyone loves our Tuscan vegetable soup, and it is a tradition in Italy. It's nutritious, hearty, and full of flavor.

Drizzle of extra-virgin olive oil
2 onions, finely chopped
2 zucchini, finely chopped
2 celery stalks, finely chopped
5 carrots, peeled and diced
5 garlic cloves, finely chopped
4 cups borlotti beans
4 cups cannellini beans
4 cups tomato puree
1 tbsp. tomato paste
8 cups chopped tomatoes (about 3½ lb.)
5 large potatoes, peeled and cubed
1 savoy cabbage, sliced
1 cup vegetable stock
Salt and pepper
Pinch of red pepper flakes
2 cups grated Parmigiano Reggiano

In a large pot over medium-high heat, add extra-virgin olive oil. Add the onions, zucchini, celery, and carrots. Cook for 8-10 minutes. Then add the chopped garlic and cook for 1 minute.

Add the borlotti beans, cannellini beans, tomato puree, tomato paste, chopped tomatoes, and potatoes. Bring to a boil and cook for about 20 minutes.

Add the savoy cabbage and the vegetable stock. Season with salt and pepper to taste and add a pinch of red pepper flakes. Then simmer for at least 1 hour.

Serve hot with a generous sprinkle of Parmigiano Reggiano on top. This is perfect with our warm, crusty Tuscan bread (see index).

Serves 10-12

Pasta e Fagioli

It's hard to imagine another dish that is more typical of the Italian table. In virtually every region and province and even in some small villages, you can find a unique version of this recipe. The types of pasta and beans change from place to place, along with the ingredients that make up the broth and give it its flavor. Here is our favorite.

1 large onion, diced
2 celery stalks, diced
Extra-virgin olive oil
2 garlic cloves, finely chopped
3 (15 oz.) cans cannellini or borlotti beans, drained and rinsed
1 tbsp. tomato paste
7 cups chicken or vegetable stock
Salt and pepper
1½ cups ditalini pasta, or any short-cut pasta
Handful of fresh basil leaves
½ cup grated Parmigiano Reggiano

In a large saucepan over medium heat, sauté the onions and celery in the olive oil until soft and translucent, about 5 minutes. Add the garlic and cook for 1 more minute.

Add the beans and stir. Add the tomato paste and stock. Increase the heat to medium high and simmer for 45 minutes.

After 45 minutes, season well with salt and pepper and add the pasta. Cook for 10 minutes or until the pasta is cooked.

Once the pasta is cooked, turn off the heat and add the basil. Serve with a generous amount of Parmigiano Reggiano and warm, crusty bread.

Serves 6

Fancy Figs

Figs always remind us of summer and our childhood in Italy. We fondly remember pulling figs straight from the trees on the farm with our Nonna and sitting on the grass, eating them together. The sweetness of the gorgonzola and figs, the sharpness of the balsamic vinegar, the saltiness of the prosciutto, and the crunch of the walnuts make this a well-balanced dish. It is simple to prepare and cook, yet tastes absolutely delicious.

4 ripe but firm fresh figs
½ cup crumbled gorgonzola dolce cheese
4 slices prosciutto di Parma
1 cup arugula
Extra-virgin olive oil
Salt and pepper
Balsamic vinegar
¼ cup walnuts, coarsely chopped

Preheat oven to 350F.

Make a small cut at the top of each fig and push in some of the gorgonzola. Wrap each fig in a slice of prosciutto. Bake for 15 minutes. The cheese will melt and the prosciutto will be crisp.

Serve immediately on a bed of arugula dressed in extra-virgin olive oil and seasoned with salt and pepper. Drizzle the balsamic vinegar over the top and sprinkle on the walnuts.

Serves 4

Passionate Penne all'Arrabbiata

This recipe celebrates the fiery passion that all Italians have. **Arrabbiata** *means "angry," and this favorite Italian dish is hot, is quick to make, and has a great depth of flavor.*

2 cups penne pasta
Extra-virgin olive oil
5 garlic cloves, finely chopped
2 cups tomato puree
3 tbsp. tomato paste
1 tbsp. red pepper flakes
Salt and pepper
Fresh basil leaves, chopped
Grated Parmigiano Reggiano

Bring a large pot of salted water to a boil, then add the pasta. Always remember that the water should be as salty as the Mediterranean Sea. Cook the pasta until al dente.

In a large skillet over medium heat, add the olive oil and then the garlic. Cook for 1 minute, stirring, until golden. Add the tomato puree, tomato paste, red pepper flakes, and salt and pepper. Bring to a boil and cook for 10 minutes. Remove from heat and add the chopped basil.

Drain the pasta, add it to the sauce, and mix well. Always do it this way and never serve the pasta with the sauce just on top! The pasta and sauce need to be combined well in the pan where the sauce was cooked, to get the best flavor. Add Parmigiano Reggiano generously on top and garnish with extra basil.

Serves 2-4

Spaghetti and Meatballs

"It's an Italian thing!"

Italian food is the most romantic in the world. This recipe was passed down from our Nonna and is a family tradition. This is such a classic dish around the world. We are famous for our Italian meatballs. Who doesn't love spaghetti and meatballs? There's a reason it's such a classic.

SAUCE

Drizzle of extra-virgin olive oil
5 garlic cloves, finely chopped
6 cups crushed tomatoes
½ cup tomato paste
Salt and pepper
¼ cup fresh basil leaves, finely chopped
1 lb. spaghetti
2 cups grated Parmigiano Reggiano

MEATBALLS

½ lb. ground beef
½ lb. ground pork
½ lb. ground veal
1 cup grated pecorino Romano
4 garlic cloves, finely chopped
1 cup breadcrumbs
2 large eggs
¼ cup fresh basil leaves, finely chopped
¼ cup fresh parsley, finely chopped
2 tsp. ground nutmeg
Salt and pepper

In a large saucepan, add extra-virgin olive oil. Add the chopped garlic and cook until golden. Add the crushed tomatoes and tomato paste, stir well, and simmer for 45 minutes. Season with salt and pepper, add the chopped basil, and stir.

In a large bowl, using your hands, mix all the meatball ingredients together well. The mixture should be soft but not too wet.

Shape the mixture into balls, and place each meatball on a tray to rest. Once all meatballs are assembled, add them straight into the sauce one at a time. They should be fully submerged in the sauce. Let them simmer in the sauce for at least 2 hours until ready to serve.

Bring a large pot of salted water to a boil. Add the spaghetti and cook until al dente. Don't just cook according to the time on the package. Scoop some out while it is cooking and taste it yourself—that's how you know when it's ready. Drain, add to the sauce, and mix well. Serve with a generous amount of Parmigiano Reggiano.

Serves 4-6

Spaghetti Aglio, Olio, e Peperoncino

This is probably one of the most popular recipes for native Italians. They like to eat it at any time, but it's best as the prime dish of a midnight feast, when they arrive home late and hungry. This is quick and simple to make and very satisfying. If you don't want any heat, don't add the chili or red pepper flakes (peperoncini).

1 lb. spaghetti or linguine
Extra-virgin olive oil
5 garlic cloves, finely chopped
1 small red chili, finely chopped with seeds, or red pepper flakes
Salt and pepper
Small bunch of flat-leaf parsley, finely chopped

Bring a large pot of salted water to a boil. Add pasta and cook until al dente.

Heat the olive oil gently in a deep skillet. Cook the garlic and chili until the garlic is golden.

Drain the pasta well, reserving a little of the cooking water, and add the pasta to the pan. Season with salt and pepper, and add 1-2 tbsp. of the pasta water if needed. Mix well and serve with parsley sprinkled on top.

Serves 4

Lemon Linguine

"When life gives you lemons . . . make lemon linguine!"

This super simple, light and fresh, lemony pasta is perfect for summer.

1 lb. spaghetti
⅔ cup extra-virgin olive oil
⅔ cup grated Parmigiano Reggiano
½ cup fresh lemon juice (about 3 lemons)
1 tbsp. lemon zest
⅓ cup fresh basil leaves, chopped
Salt and pepper
Basil and grated Parmigiano Reggiano for garnish

Cook the pasta in a large pot of boiling salted water until al dente. Meanwhile, in a large skillet over low heat, whisk together the olive oil, Parmigiano Reggiano, lemon juice, lemon zest, and basil until well combined. Remove from heat.

Drain the pasta and add to skillet with the lemon sauce. Season with salt and pepper and toss together well. Add extra basil on top, generously grate extra Parmigiano Reggiano over the top, and serve.

Serves 4

MEAT SAUCE

Extra-virgin olive oil
1 large onion, finely chopped
1 large carrot, peeled and grated
1 celery stalk, finely chopped
1 lb. ground beef
Salt and pepper
1 cup Italian red wine
3 cups tomato puree
3 tbsp. tomato paste
10 fresh basil leaves, coarsely chopped

BECHAMEL SAUCE

1 stick butter
1 cup all-purpose flour
4 cups whole milk
1 cup grated Parmigiano Reggiano
1 tsp. freshly grated nutmeg
Salt and pepper

LASAGNA

Fresh or no-boil lasagna sheets
1 cup grated Parmigiano Reggiano
1 cup grated pecorino Romano
2 cups shredded mozzarella
2 cups ricotta

Forza Four-Cheese Lasagna

Feast your eyes on the finest Italian lasagna ever! It's indulgent, rich, very cheesy, and lots of fun to make. This recipe has been handed down in the Alberti family for generations.

First make the meat sauce. In a large saucepan over medium heat, add the olive oil. Cook the onion, carrot, and celery for 5 minutes, stirring occasionally with a wooden spoon.

Add the ground beef and cook for 5 more minutes, stirring constantly, until browned all over. Season with salt and pepper, and cook for 5 more minutes.

Pour in the wine, stir well, and cook for 5 minutes until the alcohol has evaporated. Add the tomato puree, tomato paste, and basil. Reduce the heat to low and cook, uncovered, for about 2 hours, stirring occasionally, until you get a beautiful, rich sauce. Taste and season with more salt and pepper if needed.

Preheat oven to 350F.

Meanwhile, to make the béchamel sauce, melt the butter in a large saucepan over medium heat. Stir in the flour and cook for 1 minute until it becomes light brown in color. Gradually whisk in the milk. Reduce the heat to low and cook for 10 minutes, whisking constantly.

Once the sauce has thickened, stir in the cheese and nutmeg. Season with salt and pepper and set aside to cool slightly.

To assemble the lasagna, cover the bottom of a 13x9 baking dish with a little of the meat sauce. Arrange sheets of lasagna over the top (it is not necessary to cook the sheets first), then more meat sauce, then some béchamel, then some grated Parmigiano Reggiano, pecorino Romano, mozzarella, and ricotta. Continue to make layers like this until you have used all the ingredients, ending with a topping of béchamel sauce and Parmigiano Reggiano, pecorino Romano, mozzarella, and ricotta.

Bake for 35 40 minutes until golden brown. Let the dish rest for a good 10 minutes before serving, allowing the layers to firm up slightly and become easier to cut neatly.

Serves 6

Catchy Cacio e Pepe

Cacio e pepe, an old Italian favorite, is a taste of Rome. It is simple and quick and, if done our way, will capture your heart forever.

1 lb. spaghetti
1 stick butter
Pepper
1 cup grated pecorino Romano
Salt

Bring a large pot of salted water to a boil. Add pasta and cook until al dente. Drain, reserving ¾ cup pasta water.

Meanwhile, in a large heavy skillet over medium heat, melt the butter. Add a generous amount of pepper and cook, swirling the pan, for about 1 minute.

Add ½ cup reserved pasta water and bring to a simmer. Add pasta. Reduce heat to low and add pecorino Romano, stirring and tossing pasta with tongs until cheese has melted.

Remove pan from heat, season with salt, and continue stirring and tossing until sauce coats the pasta. (Add more pasta water if needed.) Transfer pasta to warm bowls and serve.

Serves 4

Saucy Spaghetti alla Puttanesca

We love to hear the many different stories behind this recipe, but this one is our favorite. **Puttanesca** *literally translates to "in the style of prostitutes," supposedly because the pungent aromas of garlic, anchovies, capers, and olives tossed with pasta were how Neapolitan prostitutes would lead customers to their doors. Very clever, if you ask us! The way to a man's heart (and wallet) is food. This spicy dish is sure to get the fire started in the kitchen and in the bedroom.*

1 lb. spaghetti
Extra-virgin olive oil
5 garlic cloves, thinly sliced
5 anchovy fillets, chopped
1 tbsp. red pepper flakes
⅓ cup coarsely chopped pitted black and green olives
2 tbsp. capers
1 cup tomato puree
3 tbsp. tomato paste
Salt and pepper
Small bunch of flat-leaf parsley, coarsely chopped

Bring a large pot of salted water to a boil. Add pasta and cook until al dente.

In a large skillet over medium-low heat, add the oil. Cook the garlic very gently until just beginning to color, then add the anchovies and stir to dissolve. Stir in the pepper flakes, then the olives and capers. Increase the heat slightly until you can hear them sizzling.

Add the tomato puree and paste and stir well. Simmer for about 10 minutes. Season with salt and pepper.

Drain the pasta, then tip into the skillet with the sauce. Toss well to combine and top with fresh parsley.

Serves 4

Racy Rigatoni

Fall-apart beef develops in flavor as you leave it to slowly cook away while you're off romancing your loved one or simply having an espresso or glass of vino! This dish also works well with pork, chicken, or lamb. The meat will end up as tender, juicy fillets, partially flaking away into the sauce and enhancing its flavor. You can also chop the fillets into large chunks before adding them to the sauce, instead of adding them whole and serving with the pasta.

Extra-virgin olive oil
5 garlic cloves, finely chopped
5 cups tomato puree
3 tbsp. tomato paste
Salt and pepper
10 fresh basil leaves, finely chopped
5 fresh sage leaves, finely chopped
4 filet mignon steaks
1 lb. rigatoni
Grated Parmigiano Reggiano

In a large, deep skillet over low heat, add the oil. Cook the garlic for a few minutes until golden.

Stir in the tomato puree and tomato paste, and season with salt and pepper. Add the basil and sage, and mix well. Add the fillets one at a time and submerge in the sauce. Simmer gently for 3 hours, until the sauce has reduced and thickened.

Once cooked, remove from the stove, taste, and season with salt and pepper again if needed. When ready to serve, bring a large pot of salted water to a boil. Add the pasta and cook until al dente.

Remove the fillets from the sauce and serve on a separate dish at the table. By this time, they will have flavored the sauce and added richness. Parts of the fillets will have flaked off into the sauce.

Drain the pasta, then add the pasta to the pan with the sauce. Toss to combine well. Serve with a generous amount of Parmigiano Reggiano.

Serves 4-6

SAUCE

6 Italian sausages
Extra-virgin olive oil
1 white onion, finely chopped
5 garlic cloves, finely chopped
1 tbsp. fennel seeds
2 bay leaves
1 cup Italian red wine
4 cups tomato puree
3 tbsp. tomato paste
Grated Parmigiano Reggiano
Fresh basil leaves

GNOCCHI

2 lb. potatoes
3 cups all-purpose flour
1 tbsp. salt

Gorgeous Gnocchi

The inclusion of fennel seeds is typically Tuscan and adds great depth and flavor to the dish. Instead of buying ground pork or sausage meat, Italians usually split sausages open and use the meat inside. Making gnocchi is great fun, and the whole family can get involved.

For the sauce, bring a large pot of salted water to a boil. Meanwhile, remove the sausages from their casings and break meat up into smaller pieces. In a skillet over medium heat, add the olive oil and onion. Cook for about 2 minutes, then add the garlic and cook until golden. Stir in the fennel seeds and bay leaves. Add the meat to the pan and cook for 6-7 minutes, or until it is cooked through. Using a wooden spoon, finely break up the meat.

Add the wine and let it reduce for a couple of minutes. Then add the tomato puree and tomato paste and mix well. Reduce the heat to low and allow the sauce to simmer for 45 minutes.

To make the gnocchi, peel the potatoes and cook in a large pot of boiling salted water until tender. Drain and pass them through a *passatutto* or ricer into a bowl, or mash well to a smooth consistency. Add 1 cup flour and the salt to form a soft, pliable dough.

Pour the remaining flour in a mound on a work surface, and turn the dough out onto the flour. Knead the flour into the dough, adding a little more if the dough sticks to your hands. The more flour you add at this stage, the heavier the gnocchi will be, so try not to add too much.

You need to decide how big to make the gnocchi. The trick is to keep them the same size so that they have the same cooking time. Roll the dough out into long sausages and chop into pieces between 1 and 1½ inches in length. You can then roll them over the tines of a fork for texture or use a gnocchi board, so that more sauce will stick to them. But you can leave them simply pillow shaped and plain.

Bring a large pot of salted water to a boil and drop in the gnocchi. They are cooked when they bob back up to the surface—this takes 2-4 minutes. Drain well and toss with the sauce in the skillet. Serve with Parmigiano Reggiano and fresh basil leaves sprinkled on top.

Serves 4-6

Gnocchi con Pollo e Funghi

This dish combines gnocchi with chicken and mushrooms in a beautiful cream sauce. Very easy and quick to make, this is comfort food at its best—indulgent, delicious, and filling, yet it always leaves you wanting more. . . .

Extra-virgin olive oil
10 oz. chicken breast, diced
5 garlic cloves, finely chopped
10 fresh porcini mushrooms, sliced
1 stick butter
1 cup heavy cream
2 tbsp. dried thyme
2 tbsp. dried sage
2 tbsp. dried rosemary
Salt and pepper
1 lb. gnocchi
1 cup grated Parmigiano Reggiano

Drizzle a little extra-virgin olive oil in a large skillet. Add the chicken and cook until done, about 10 minutes. Add the garlic and cook until golden.

Add the mushrooms and butter, and cook for a few more minutes. Now add the cream, dried thyme, sage, and rosemary, and mix well. Simmer for 5 minutes and season well with salt and pepper.

Cook the gnocchi in a large pot of boiling salted water. You will know the gnocchi are ready when they start to rise to the top. Drain the gnocchi and add to the pan with the sauce. Add the Parmigiano Reggiano and mix well. Serve and enjoy.

Serves 4

The Cheesiest, Creamiest, Dreamiest Mac and Cheese Ever!

This dish is a mouthful . . . the ultimate comfort food at its best. Who doesn't love mac and cheese? This is our Twintastico Twist on the classic. It's creamy, it's dreamy, and you guessed it, it's cheesy—and it's the best.

2 sticks unsalted butter
6 tbsp. all-purpose flour
3 cups whole milk
1 cup heavy cream
Salt and pepper
1 tbsp. Dijon mustard
1 tsp. grated nutmeg
6 cups coarsely grated strong cheddar
1½ cups grated Parmigiano Reggiano
3 cups shredded mozzarella
2 lb. macaroni

TOPPING

1 cup breadcrumbs
1 cup grated Parmigiano Reggiano
Salt and pepper
Extra-virgin olive oil

Preheat oven to 350F. Butter a baking dish.

In a large wide pot over medium-low heat, melt the butter. Sprinkle flour over butter, whisking to incorporate and make a roux. Cook, stirring constantly with a wooden spoon, until roux is light golden, about 4 minutes.

Gradually pour in milk and cream, whisking constantly to incorporate and make a béchamel sauce. Raise heat to medium-high and bring sauce to a low boil, whisking constantly. Reduce to a simmer, whisking occasionally, and cook until béchamel sauce is thick and coats the back of a spoon, about 3 minutes more.

Season with salt and pepper. Add the mustard and mix well. Add the nutmeg. Then start to add the cheeses in batches, whisking until each addition is completely melted before adding more. Remove from heat.

Bring a large pot of salted water to a boil. Add the macaroni and cook until just al dente.

Drain the macaroni and add to the pot with the cheese sauce. Stir well to coat. Transfer macaroni mixture to the buttered baking dish.

For the topping, sprinkle the breadcrumbs evenly over the macaroni, then the Parmigiano Reggiano. Season with salt and pepper and drizzle extra-virgin olive oil over the top. Bake for 15-20 minutes, until golden and bubbling.

Serves 6

Perfetto Penne alla Vodka

This is more an American-Italian recipe than an Italian-American one. It is very simple to make and we love the creaminess of the dish. We like the sauce a little fiery, so we're generous with the peperoncini. You can add as much or as little as you like.

Extra-virgin olive oil
1 large white onion, finely chopped
Red pepper flakes
5 garlic cloves, finely chopped
½ cup vodka
2 cups tomato puree
1 tbsp. tomato paste
1 cup heavy cream
Salt and pepper
1 lb. penne pasta
1 cup grated Parmigiano Reggiano
10 fresh basil leaves, finely chopped

In a large skillet over medium heat, add the olive oil and onions. Cook until soft. Then add the pepper flakes and garlic, and cook until garlic is golden. Pour in the vodka and cook 2-3 minutes to reduce.

Pour in the tomato puree and tomato paste, and stir until thoroughly combined. Reduce the heat to low and simmer for 15-20 minutes. Now it's time to add the heavy cream. Stir to combine, and simmer for 5 more minutes. Season with salt and pepper to taste.

Bring a large pot of salted water to a boil. Cook pasta until al dente; drain.

Pour the drained pasta into the sauce and toss to combine. Sprinkle on the Parmigiano Reggiano and basil, mix together well, and serve.

Serves 4-6

Sexy Spirali Pasta

Here is a simple, colorful, summery recipe that everyone will enjoy. Adding the crispy, salty pancetta and the sweet peas makes this a tasty, quick, and perfect dish.

1 lb. spirali pasta or any short pasta
Drizzle of extra-virgin olive oil
1½ cups cubed pancetta
1 cup frozen peas
Salt and pepper
1 stick butter, sliced in pieces
Grated Parmigiano Reggiano

Bring a pot of salted water to a boil. Add the pasta, and cook until al dente. To a preheated, deep skillet, add a little drizzle of extra-virgin olive oil and the pancetta, and cook until crisp.

Once the pancetta is nearly cooked, add the peas, salt, and pepper. Cook for 5 more minutes.

When the pasta is ready, drain and add it to the pan with the pancetta and peas. Add the butter and mix well. Serve with a generous sprinkle of Parmigiano Reggiano.

Serves 4-6

Italian Stallion Pasta Bake

We love a pasta bake in our family. You can always make a big batch to feed everyone, and Italians love to eat! Filling, and packed with amazing flavor and ingredients, this is the real deal Italian Stallion pasta bake.

Extra-virgin olive oil
2 lb. Italian sausages
1 large onion, finely chopped
5 garlic cloves, finely chopped
5 cups tomato puree
1 tbsp. tomato paste
Salt and pepper
1 cup fresh spinach
10 fresh basil leaves
2 lb. rigatoni
5 cups sliced mozzarella
1 cup grated Parmigiano Reggiano

In a skillet over medium heat, add the olive oil. Take the casings off the sausages, and add meat to skillet. Break up with wooden spoon into thick chunks. Cook for about 8 minutes. Add the onions and cook until translucent, about 5 minutes. Add the garlic and cook until golden.

Add the tomato puree and tomato paste, and season with salt and pepper. Mix well. Chop the spinach and basil and add to the skillet. Mix well and reduce heat. As the sauce simmers, bring a large pot of salted water to a boil. Add the rigatoni and cook until al dente.

Preheat oven to 350F.

Drain the rigatoni and add to the skillet with the sausages and sauce. Mix well, then lightly oil a 14x10-inch baking dish. Spread the pasta mixture in the baking dish, then break up the mozzarella and spread it around the top of the dish. Cover with Parmigiano Reggiano. Bake until the sauce is bubbling, the Parmigiano is nice and crispy on top, and the mozzarella is melted, 20-25 minutes.

Serves 8

Magnifico Melanzane

*This classic recipe from Sicily, **parmigiana di melanzane**, is a true delight. Done our way, this dish will have your mouth watering.*

Extra-virgin olive oil
1 large onion, finely chopped
5 garlic cloves, thinly sliced
3 cups tomato puree
3 tbsp. tomato paste
15 fresh basil leaves, finely chopped
5 fresh sage leaves, finely chopped
Salt and pepper
2 large eggplants, cut into ½-inch slices, stems removed
1 cup grated Parmigiano Reggiano
1 lb. ball fresh mozzarella, thinly sliced
½ cup breadcrumbs

Preheat oven to 350F.

In a large saucepan, heat the olive oil over medium heat. Add the onions and cook for about 5 minutes. Then add the garlic and cook until golden.

Add the tomato puree, tomato paste, basil, and sage. Mix well and bring to a boil, stirring often. Reduce the heat and simmer for 45 minutes. Season with salt and pepper.

Heat a griddle pan over high heat. Brush the eggplant slices with olive oil, then in batches, griddle on both sides until soft and lightly charred. Remove from the griddle and set aside.

In a 14x10 baking dish, place a thin layer of tomato sauce in the bottom. Then sprinkle with a little of the grated Parmigiano Reggiano. Place a layer of the eggplant on top and season with salt and pepper.

Repeat the layers, finishing with the tomato sauce. Sprinkle a generous amount of Parmigiano Reggiano over the top. Tear the mozzarella and scatter on top. Scatter on the breadcrumbs. Bake for 40 minutes or until bubbling and golden brown. Remove from the oven and allow to stand for 5 minutes before serving.

Serves 6

FILLING

2 cups fresh spinach
1½ cups ricotta
1 egg yolk
Salt and pepper

PASTA DOUGH

4 cups 00 flour
4 large eggs
Extra flour for dusting
Egg wash

SAUCE

Extra-virgin olive oil
1 stick butter
2 shallots, finely chopped
1 cup Italian white wine
1 cup heavy cream
2 cups grated Parmigiano Reggiano
10 fresh sage leaves, finely chopped
½ cup walnuts, coarsely chopped
Salt and pepper

Spectacular Spinach and Ricotta Ravioli

This is a firm favorite in Casa Alberti: rich, indulgent, and delicious. This warming, beautifully creamy, well-balanced dish will be sure to put a big smile on your face.

To make the filling, place the spinach in a large saucepan with a lid, and cover with a little water. Steam, covered, for about 5 minutes, until the spinach has wilted. Remove from the heat, drain, and allow to cool.

When the spinach is cool enough to handle, squeeze out the water. Finely chop the spinach, then combine in a mixing bowl with the ricotta and egg yolk. Season with salt and pepper, and mix well.

To make the pasta, place the flour on a board or in a bowl and make a well in the center. Crack the eggs into the well. Then with a fork, mix the eggs into the flour as much as possible so it's not sticky. Don't worry if there are lumps in the dough; keep mixing until crumbs form.

Put on a flat surface and knead crumbs together until you have a silky-smooth, elastic dough. You are aiming to achieve a Play-Doh-like texture. Cover with plastic wrap and chill for 30 minutes in the fridge.

Divide the dough into 2 balls, and squash them flat with your fingers. Keep 1 piece covered with plastic wrap, so it doesn't get dry and crusty. If you are using a pasta roller, roll the other piece through on the thickest setting.

Fold into thirds, then repeat 5 times. Once you have a rough square shape, start working it through the machine, taking it down one setting at a time until you have reached the thinnest setting. If your pasta is too sticky, it won't go through smoothly, so add a little flour to each side before you put it through the roller.

Repeat with the other piece. You should end up with 2 long sheets of pasta. You can also roll this by hand using a rolling pin, but you'll need some serious elbow grease to get your pasta sheets really thin and wide (about 1 playing card thick and 3-4 inches wide). But it is good fun to do with children and they really do enjoy rolling out the pasta with the rolling pin.

Lay the pasta out flat on a floured surface. Down the center of 1 pasta sheet, place spoonfuls of the filling 2 inches apart. Brush egg wash around each spoonful of filling. Lay the other pasta sheet on top, and press around each spoonful of filling to seal, making sure all air is pushed out. Using a pasta cutter, cut squares or circles around the filling.

Bring a large pot of salted water to a boil. Reduce to a gentle boil. Very gently lower the ravioli into the boiling water. Cook for 1-2 minutes or until the ravioli float to the top and are tender. Don't let the water boil too vigorously, as this may cause the ravioli to split.

To make the sauce, in a large skillet, heat a little extra-virgin olive oil and the butter. Cook the shallots for a few minutes, then add the white wine and simmer for 5 minutes. Add the cream, Parmigiano Reggiano, sage, walnuts, salt, and pepper, and reduce for 15 minutes over medium heat. Drain the ravioli, add to the pan with the sauce, and mix well. Serve immediately, adding extra walnuts on top and a good sprinkling of Parmigiano Reggiano to finish.

Serves 6

Tantalizing Tagliatelle with Italian Sausage in a Creamy Leek Sauce

"Everyone loves an Italian sausage."

This is a beautiful dish packed full of delicious flavor. Always use Italian sausages in this recipe. You will know they are Italian sausages because they are bigger and better than the rest!

Extra-virgin olive oil
2 shallots, finely chopped
2 large leeks
1 lb. Italian sausages
½ cup Italian white wine
1 cup heavy cream
Salt and pepper
8 fresh sage leaves, finely chopped
3 sprigs fresh thyme
1 lb. tagliatelle

In a large skillet over medium heat, add extra-virgin olive oil. Add the chopped shallots, and cook for about 3 minutes. Slice the leeks into thin discs, about ½ inch thick. Add to the pan and cook for another 5 minutes.

Slit the sausages lengthwise, peel off the casings, and break meat into small, equal pieces. Add to the pan and cook for 8-10 minutes. Then add the white wine and reduce for about 5 minutes.

Add the heavy cream, and season with salt and pepper. Add the sage and thyme, mix well, and reduce for another 10 minutes.

Bring a large pot of salted water to a boil. Cook the pasta until al dente. Drain, add to skillet with the sausage and leek cream sauce, and mix well. Serve immediately.

Serves 4

Twintastico Tagliatelle al Ragu

"We like our wine like we like our women . . . Italian, strong, and full bodied."

Now this is our family recipe, and we do it our way! It is one of our favorite dishes to make. It tastes amazing and is sure to bring the whole family around as it is cooking. The sauce should simmer for at least 3 hours to develop its deep, rich flavors. For us, if the wine isn't good enough to drink, it isn't good enough to go in our sauce. Use tagliatelle pasta with this dish, as it holds the sauce a lot better than spaghetti. This is our Sunday sauce!

Extra-virgin olive oil
5 garlic cloves, finely chopped
½ lb. ground beef
½ lb. ground pork
1 cup Italian red wine
1 tbsp. tomato paste
5 cups tomato puree
Salt and pepper
10 fresh basil leaves, finely chopped
1 lb. tagliatelle
Grated Parmigiano Reggiano

In a large skillet, heat the oil over medium-low heat. Cook the garlic for a few minutes until golden. Crumble the meat between your fingertips, add to the pan, and cook until brown—about 10 minutes. Add the red wine and simmer for another 5 minutes until it has reduced.

Now stir in the tomato paste and tomato puree. Season with salt and pepper. Add the basil and simmer gently for 3 hours until reduced and thickened, stirring occasionally. This gives you plenty of time to have an espresso or glass of wine and romance your loved one while you wait!

Once cooked, remove from the heat, taste, and season with salt and pepper again if needed.

When ready to serve, bring a large pot of salted water to a boil. Add the pasta and cook until al dente. Drain the pasta, add to the pan with the sauce, and toss to combine well. The pasta and sauce need to be mixed well together in the pan where the sauce was cooked to get the best flavor. Serve with a generous amount of Parmigiano Reggiano.

Serves 4

Risotto ai Funghi

Risotto is very simple to make. A lot of people believe that it's more difficult than it really is. If you use the right ingredients, it can be the perfect, easy, creamy risotto we have all dreamed about. Various ingredients can be used in a risotto, such as meat, poultry, fish, and vegetables, but this is one of our favorites. Porcini mushrooms add that extra depth of flavor and earthiness.

⅓ cup dried porcini mushrooms
4 cups vegetable or reserved porcini stock
2 sticks butter
Drizzle of extra-virgin olive oil
6 shallots, finely chopped
5 cups Arborio rice
1 cup Italian white wine
½ cup grated Parmigiano Reggiano
Salt and pepper

Soak the dried porcini mushrooms in warm water for about 30 minutes to soften. Remove the mushrooms from the water and set aside (you can use the porcini mushroom water as stock if you want to add to the risotto).

In a large saucepan over high heat, bring stock to a boil. Reduce the heat to low and keep the stock hot.

In a large, deep, heavy saucepan over medium heat, melt the butter and drizzle in a little extra-virgin olive oil. Add shallots and cook, stirring frequently, for about 3 minutes. Add the rice and stir for a few minutes to coat with the butter.

Add the wine and simmer until most of the liquid has evaporated, about 2 minutes. Add a ladle of the stock and stir until almost completely absorbed. Now add the porcini mushrooms and mix well. Continue adding the stock a ladle at a time, stirring constantly and allowing the rice to absorb each addition of the stock before adding the next. Cook until the rice is tender but still firm to the bite and the mixture is creamy, about 20 minutes.

Remove the pan from the heat, and add the Parmigiano Reggiano. Season with salt and pepper, add extra butter, and mix well. Cover and allow to rest for 5 minutes before serving.

Serves 4

Ravishing Risotto Verde

This green risotto is not only healthy, fresh, and extremely tasty but looks stunningly beautiful and elegant, just like Italians. Very pleasing on the eyes and palate!

Extra-virgin olive oil
2 sticks butter
6 shallots, diced
1 celery stalk, diced
Salt
4 cups Arborio rice
1 cup Italian white wine
4 cups vegetable stock, hot
1 cup fresh spinach
⅓ cup fresh basil leaves
⅓ cup frozen peas
Pepper
1 cup grated Parmigiano Reggiano
2 tbsp. mascarpone
Zest and juice of 1 lemon
Micro cress

In a skillet over medium heat, add the oil and butter. Add the shallots and celery with a little salt. Cook for 5 minutes until translucent.

Add the rice and stir well, ensuring that every grain is coated. Pour in the wine and let it bubble until it's almost all evaporated. Add the stock a ladleful at a time, stirring constantly and adding more stock only when the last ladleful has been absorbed.

In a food processor, puree the spinach and basil with 2 tbsp. hot water. Once the rice is almost cooked and all stock used, stir in the puree and add the peas. Cook for another 5 minutes, stirring frequently. Season with salt and pepper.

Once the rice and vegetables are cooked, stir in the Parmigiano Reggiano, mascarpone, lemon zest, and a squeeze of juice. Season again, and top with micro cress before serving.

Serves 4

Classic Carbonara

Now in the authentic carbonara, no cream or milk is used. A lot of people make this mistake. We add an extra yolk to achieve more creaminess without the cream. This dish was brought to Lazio from Umbria by coal workers (carbonari), who came to sell charcoal to the Romans. The Romans adopted it, and it is now famous worldwide. Guanciale (Italian cured pork cheek) is traditionally used in this recipe, but if you can't get hold of it, pancetta is fine to use.

4 eggs
1 egg yolk
½ cup grated Parmigiano Reggiano or pecorino Romano
Salt and pepper
1 lb. spaghetti
1 cup diced guanciale or pancetta

Place the eggs in a bowl. Add the Parmigiano Reggiano or pecorino Romano, and season with salt and pepper. Mix well with a fork and set aside. Cook the pasta in a large pot of boiling salted water until al dente.

Meanwhile, in a large skillet over high heat, cook the guanciale or pancetta until crisp. When the pasta is ready, drain and add to the pan with the guanciale. Mix well, then take off the heat! That is a very important part here: you don't want the pan hot, as this will scramble the eggs when you add them. Add the egg and cheese mixture and stir to coat the pasta. Serve immediately with extra cheese and pepper to taste.

Serves 4

Spaghetti con Frutti di Mare

Seafood pastas are staples of Italian gastronomy but vary enormously in Italy from region to region. The most important thing to remember is that the seafood must be the freshest possible. We love our spaghetti and we love our fish, so this is a match made in heaven.

1 lb. spaghetti
Extra-virgin olive oil
4 garlic cloves, finely chopped
2 lb. mixed fresh seafood such as mussels, shrimp, calamari, scallops, salmon, etc.
Red pepper flakes
1 cup dry Italian white wine
Salt and pepper
Large bunch of flat-leaf parsley, chopped

Add the spaghetti to a pot of salted boiling water and cook until al dente. In a large pan over medium-low heat, add the olive oil. Add the garlic and cook until golden. Pour in the seafood and stir until cooked.

Add the red pepper flakes to the pan, then add the white wine. Simmer, letting it reduce. Drain the spaghetti, add to the pan with the seafood, and mix well. Cook in the pan for another 2-3 minutes. Season with salt and pepper, add the parsley, mix well, and serve.

Serves 4

Spaghetti alle Vongole

This light, yet flavorful dish is an Italian classic that we love: pasta infused with garlic, briny clams, white wine, and chili.

Extra-virgin olive oil
3 garlic cloves, thinly sliced
1 tsp. red pepper flakes or 2 red chilies, finely chopped
2 lb. clams in shells
1 cup Italian white wine
1 lb. spaghetti
Flat-leaf parsley
Salt and pepper

Drizzle a little extra-virgin olive oil into a large pan. Add the garlic and chilies, then cook gently until golden. Add the clams and the white wine and bring to a boil. Cover the pan and cook for about 5 minutes, until the clams are open. Give the pan a shake, and discard any clams that do not open.

Cook spaghetti in a large pot of salted water until al dente. Drain the pasta, then tip into the pan with the clams. Add the parsley, season with salt and pepper, and toss together.

Serves 4

Mamma's Spaghetti al Pomodoro

"Just like Mamma used to make it."

We are very much **Mammoni** *(Italian for "Mamma's boys"). Our Mamma will always be the heart of the family home. She has raised us to be the men we are today and has provided for us the only way an Italian Mamma can, with love and affection. This recipe is a favorite in our house and used a lot for "Spaghetti Sunday." It is fresh and easy and the whole family will love it. Making pasta sauce, in fact, is really simple, and you can prepare it in no time at all.* **Ti vogliamo tanto bene, Mamma.**

1 lb. spaghetti or bucatini
Extra-virgin olive oil
5 garlic cloves, finely chopped
5 cups tomato puree
1 tbsp. tomato paste
10 fresh basil leaves, finely chopped
6 fresh sage leaves, finely chopped
Salt and pepper
1 cup grated Parmigiano Reggiano or pecorino Romano

Bring a pan of salted water to a boil for the pasta—remember, salty as the Mediterranean Sea! While that's happening, in a large skillet, add the oil and cook garlic until golden. Then add the tomato puree, tomato paste, and chopped basil and sage. Season with salt and pepper and stir. Simmer for about 45 minutes until the sauce reduces and thickens. Taste the sauce and season with salt and pepper if needed.

Add the pasta to the pot of water and cook until al dente. Drain the pasta and add to the pan with the sauce. Mix together for 1-2 minutes to let the pasta absorb the sauce.

Always mix the pasta with the sauce and never, ever just put the sauce on top of the pasta. It won't combine with and coat the pasta and is not the Italian way. Please don't do this—it upsets us very much! Sprinkle with grated Parmigiano Reggiano or pecorino Romano and serve immediately.

Serves 4

Secondi

Secondi are meat, poultry, fish, or vegetable main dishes that follow after *primi*. With meat dishes we like to have a nice glass or two of **vino rosso**, and with fish dishes **vino bianco**. Here you will find some of our family's favorite recipes and some Italian Twintastico Twists along the way. *Salute.*

Only two things improve with age . . . Italians and wine.

Nonna Maria's Chicken Cutlets

This recipe brings back fond memories of our childhood. We remember running home from school, knowing our Nonna would be in the kitchen cooking for us when we arrived. We remember the smells coming from the kitchen as we opened the door and saw our Nonna in her apron at the stove. These are beautiful childhood memories we will never forget and are so grateful for.

4 skinless boneless chicken breasts
1 cup all-purpose flour
2 large eggs
1 cup breadcrumbs
1 tbsp. dried sage, optional
Vegetable oil for frying
2 garlic cloves
Salt and pepper
1 lemon

Place the chicken breasts on a board and cut in half lengthwise. Cover with a double layer of plastic wrap. Bash with a saucepan—or Nonna's favorite, a rolling pin—to flatten them to around ¼ inch thick.

Add the flour to a bowl, then crack and beat the eggs in a second bowl. Add the breadcrumbs to a third bowl and mix in the dried sage, if desired.

Coat the chicken in the flour, then the egg, and finally in the breadcrumbs, until thoroughly coated.

In a large, deep skillet, heat the oil over medium heat. Add the whole garlic cloves. Cook the chicken for 3-4 minutes on each side, or until the cutlets are golden and cooked through. Season with salt and pepper and serve with a squeeze of lemon.

Serves 4

Seductive Saltimbocca

*Saltimbocca **means** "jumps in the mouth" **in Italian. And this dish does just that!** **Traditionally done with veal, our recipe uses chicken, but you could use pork also.***

2 skinless boneless chicken breasts
Salt and pepper
8 slices prosciutto di Parma
8 fresh sage leaves
Extra-virgin olive oil
¼ cup marsala or Italian white wine
1 stick butter

Cut each chicken breast in half lengthwise to make 4 fillets. Cover with plastic wrap and, using a meat mallet or rolling pin, pound until chicken is about ½ inch thick. Season both sides with salt and pepper.

Place 2 slices of prosciutto di Parma on top of each chicken piece. Top each with 2 sage leaves and weave a toothpick through to secure them in place.

In a skillet, heat the oil over medium heat. Cook the chicken for about 2 minutes on each side, until cooked through. Transfer to serving plates.

Add the marsala or white wine to the oil in the pan, and reduce over high heat for 2 minutes. Add the butter. Return the saltimbocca and any juices to the pan, turning them in the sauce for about 1 minute. Remove the pan from the heat and remove the toothpicks from the saltimbocca. Serve with juices drizzled over.

Serves 4

Pollo al Marsala

This simple, classic chicken dish originates from Marsala, Sicily. This recipe uses very few ingredients but the result is rich and full of flavor.

½ cup all-purpose flour
Salt and pepper
4 skinless boneless chicken breasts
Extra-virgin olive oil
2 shallots, thinly sliced
1 cup sliced porcini mushrooms
1 cup marsala wine
2 cups tomato puree
⅔ cup butter

Put the flour on a large plate and season with salt and pepper. Dip the chicken breasts in the seasoned flour to coat.

In a large skillet, heat the oil over medium-high heat. Add the chicken and cook for 2 minutes each side or until lightly browned. Remove the chicken from the pan and set aside.

Reduce the heat to medium. Add the shallots and mushrooms to the oil in the pan, and cook for 5 minutes or until softened, stirring occasionally. Increase the heat and pour in the marsala. Bring to a boil and let it bubble for 2 minutes.

Stir in the tomato puree and butter. Season with salt and pepper. Reduce the heat to medium low, return the chicken to the pan, and cook gently for 20 minutes. Check for seasoning and serve immediately with mixed vegetables or roast potatoes.

Serves 4

Pesce Pesce

Pesce means fish in Italian. Our Twintastico fish dish with tomatoes, olives, and capers is fresh, light, easy, and delicious.

Extra-virgin olive oil
1 large white onion, finely chopped
5 garlic cloves, finely chopped
5 cups tomato puree or chopped tomatoes
¼ cup tomato paste
1 cup black olives, halved
¼ cup capers
Generous pinch of red pepper flakes
2 lb. fresh cod fillets
Salt and pepper
Large bunch of flat-leaf parsley, coarsely chopped

In a large, deep skillet, heat the olive oil over medium heat. Add the onions and cook for about 5 minutes. Add the garlic and stir frequently until the garlic is golden, about 1 minute. Then add the tomato puree, tomato paste, olives, capers, and a generous pinch of red pepper flakes. Stir to combine.

Place the cod fillets in the skillet in a single layer. Nestle them into the tomato mixture and cover with sauce. Season with salt and pepper and simmer over medium-low heat for about 45 minutes. Just before serving, add the chopped parsley and combine. Place each piece of cod on a plate, top with the tomato sauce, and sprinkle extra parsley on top.

Serves 4-6

Salmon with a Pistachio, Honey, and Herb Crust

This beautiful salmon with a colorful, crunchy pistachio, honey, and herb crust is served alongside broccoli rabe with peperoncino chili and garlic.

½ cup shelled pistachios
⅓ cup breadcrumbs
1 tbsp. chopped fresh rosemary
1 tbsp. chopped fresh thyme
2 tbsp. chopped fresh flat-leaf parsley
Salt and pepper
2 tsp. honey
Extra-virgin olive oil
4 skinless salmon fillets (about 4 oz. each)
1 large bunch broccoli rabe (rapini)
½ red chili, finely chopped, or 1 tsp. red pepper flakes
2 garlic cloves, finely chopped

Preheat the oven to 375F.

Chop the pistachios very finely so they are about the same size as the breadcrumbs. Sift to remove the dusty skins. Place in a small bowl with the breadcrumbs and herbs, and season with salt and pepper. Drizzle over the honey, mix well, and set aside.

Brush a little oil over the bottom of a baking dish. Place the salmon in a dish and season with salt and pepper. Top the fillets with the pistachio mixture, pressing it down firmly with the back of a spoon. Transfer to the baking dish, drizzle with a little olive oil, and bake for 25 minutes or until the topping is golden and crisp.

Blanch the broccoli for 2 minutes in boiling salted water. Drain the broccoli, then sauté in olive oil with the chili and garlic for about 3 minutes. Serve the salmon with the broccoli and enjoy!

Serves 4

FISH

1 cup all-purpose flour
¾ cup cornstarch
1 tsp. baking powder
Salt and pepper
1¼ cups Italian beer (Peroni or Moretti)
2 tbsp. finely chopped fresh sage leaves
2 tbsp. finely chopped fresh basil leaves
2 tbsp. finely chopped flat-leaf parsley
Vegetable oil for frying
4 thick white fish fillets (7 oz. each,
preferably cod, pollock, or haddock)

CHIPS

2 lb. potatoes, peeled
4 cups vegetable oil
Salt and pepper
Truffle oil
1 cup shaved Parmigiano Reggiano

MUSHY PEAS

Extra-virgin olive oil
1 cup pancetta cubes
1½ cups frozen peas
Salt and pepper
½ stick butter

Italian Fish and Chips

Fish and chips are a British institution, and everyone loves them. American "chips" are known in Britain as "crisps." British "chips" are called "fries" in the U.S.—yes, we know it's very confusing. Fish and chips are delicious and crisp. This is our Italian version of the British classic with mushy peas.

To prepare the fish, in a large bowl, mix the flour, cornstarch, and baking powder. Season with salt and pepper.

Using a fork, and whisking continuously, add the Italian beer to the flour mixture. Continue mixing until you have a thick, smooth batter. Add the sage, basil, and parsley, and mix well. Chill the batter in the fridge for 30 minutes to 1 hour.

Heat oil in a deep fryer or large, deep skillet. Lay the fish fillets on a sheet of parchment paper and pat dry. Season with sea salt and pepper.

Dust each fish fillet with a little extra flour before dipping into the batter, and shake off any excess. Only dip the fish in the batter at the last moment before frying. This way you will always have a light and crisp snap to the cooked batter.

Dip fish into the batter, then carefully lower each fillet into the hot oil. Fry for about 8 minutes or until the batter is crisp and golden, turning the fillets from time to time with a large slotted spoon. Remove the fillets from the hot oil, drain on paper towels, cover with greaseproof paper, and keep hot.

For the chips, cut the potatoes into ½-inch slices, then slice these into ½-inch-wide sticks. Place the chips in a colander and rinse under cold running water.

Place the washed chips in a pot of cold water, bring to a gentle boil, and simmer for 3-4 minutes. Drain carefully through a colander, then dry with paper towels.

In a deep fryer or large, deep saucepan, heat the oil to 250F. Blanch the chips, a few handfuls at a time, in the oil for a couple of minutes. Do not brown them. Once the chips are slightly cooked, remove them, drain on paper towels, and set aside.

Heat the oil to 400F, then cook the chips until golden and crisp, about 5 minutes. Remove and set aside. Season with salt and pepper, drizzle truffle oil generously on top, then top with the Parmigiano Reggiano. Don't be shy with the cheese—the more the better!

To prepare the mushy peas, in a large skillet, drizzle a little extra-virgin olive oil. Add the pancetta and cook for about 5 minutes until crisp. Add the peas and season with salt and pepper. Add the butter, mix together, and cook for 5 more minutes.

Serves 4

The Biggest and Best Italian Sandwich in the World

"Mangia, mangia!"

In Casa Alberti, we always go big—bigger and better. This is why our Italian sandwich is the best in the world. All the best ingredients make this the best tasting and looking sandwich ever. Everyone wants an Alberti sandwich. Go big or go home!

1 loaf Holy Focaccia (see index)
Blessed Basil Pesto (see index)
Arugula leaves
5 slices provolone cheese
10 slices salami
10 slices prosciutto di Parma
10 slices mortadella
1 cup sliced mozzarella
3 fresh tomatoes, sliced
Salt and pepper
Drizzle of extra-virgin olive oil
Fresh basil leaves
3 garlic cloves, finely chopped
Mayonnaise

Cut the focaccia in half crosswise. Spread a generous amount of the pesto sauce on the bottom half of the focaccia. Then layer the sandwich, starting with a handful of arugula leaves, then the provolone cheese, then the slices of salami, prosciutto, mortadella, followed by the mozzarella. Season the tomatoes with salt, pepper, and extra-virgin olive oil, and place on top of the mozzarella. Add the basil leaves.

Now in a bowl, mix the garlic and mayonnaise. Spread the garlic mayonnaise generously on the top half of the focaccia, then place that half on top of the sandwich. To serve, cut the focaccia into quarters.

Makes 4 sandwiches

Italian Roast

"Everyone loves an Italian roast!"

Here is a perfect combination that everyone will enjoy: succulent lamb with Italian roast potatoes that are crispy on the outside and fluffy on the inside. The long roasting time for the lamb allows the flavors to develop and the meat to fall off the bone.

LAMB

1 whole leg of lamb
Extra-virgin olive oil
8 garlic cloves, halved
Fresh rosemary sprigs
Salt and pepper
1 tbsp. dried sage
1 tbsp. dried thyme

ROAST POTATOES

4 or 5 large potatoes
Extra-virgin olive oil
5 garlic cloves, finely chopped
Fresh rosemary, finely chopped
Fresh sage leaves, finely chopped
Salt and pepper

Remove the lamb from the refrigerator 1 hour before you want to cook it, to let it come up to room temperature.

Preheat oven to 325F.

Drizzle extra-virgin olive oil all over the lamb. Cut slits in the top of the lamb every few inches, deep enough to push the pieces of garlic and rosemary sprigs in. Season generously with salt and pepper, and sprinkle the sage and thyme all over the lamb.

Cover the lamb in foil and roast in oven for 4-5 hours, until the lamb meat begins to fall off the bone. Allow to rest for 15 minutes before serving.

While the lamb is cooking, peel the potatoes and cut into small chunks. Put in a large bowl and drizzle with extra-virgin olive oil. Add the garlic, rosemary, sage, salt, and pepper, and mix well.

Transfer the potatoes to a large baking sheet, and drizzle a little extra-virgin olive oil on top. Remove lamb from oven and tent loosely with foil to keep warm. Increase oven temperature to 375F, and put potatoes in the oven for at least 1 hour, until golden brown and crispy. Serve with the leg of lamb.

Serves 4-6

Spezzatino di Manzo con Polenta

This hearty Italian beef stew is enriched with the flavors of rosemary, sage, and thyme. Served on a creamy, dreamy bed of polenta, it is delicious!

STEW

Drizzle of extra-virgin olive oil
3 carrots, peeled and cut into ½-inch pieces
3 celery stalks, cut into ½-inch pieces
2 onions, cut into medium dice
6 garlic cloves, finely chopped
2 lb. stew beef, such as boneless chuck, cut into 2-inch cubes
2 cups Italian red wine
2 cups tomato puree or canned diced tomatoes
3 tbsp. tomato paste
8 sprigs fresh thyme
8 fresh sage leaves, finely chopped
1 tbsp. fresh rosemary, chopped
Salt and pepper

POLENTA

4 cups water
1 cup polenta
1 cup grated Parmigiano Reggiano
1 stick butter
Extra-virgin olive oil

To make the stew, in a large saucepan over medium heat, add extra-virgin olive oil and the carrots, celery, and onions. Cook, stirring, for 5 minutes. Add the garlic and cook for another 2 minutes.

Add the beef and cook for 5 minutes. Add the wine and reduce for 5 minutes. Now add the tomato puree, tomato paste, thyme, sage, and rosemary.

Bring to a boil. Season with salt and pepper, and reduce heat to low. Simmer for 3 hours or until the beef is tender and the sauce is thick.

To make the polenta, in a large saucepan, bring the water to a boil. Slowly add the polenta, stirring constantly, and reduce the heat. After a few minutes, add the Parmigiano Reggiano and butter, and mix well. Drizzle in a little extra-virgin olive oil and mix.

Serve the Italian stew on a bed of creamy polenta and enjoy.

Serves 6

SAUSAGE-IN-THE-HOLE

⅓ cup vegetable oil
8 Italian sausages
3 red onions, cut into wedges
1 tbsp. fennel seeds
2 tbsp. fresh rosemary
1 tbsp. finely chopped fresh sage leaves
2 cups all-purpose flour
4 eggs, lightly beaten
1¼ cups whole milk
Salt and pepper

SAUCE

2 shallots, thinly sliced
Extra-virgin olive oil
1 sprig fresh rosemary
2 tbsp. balsamic vinegar
1¾ cups Italian red wine
1¾ cups vegetable stock
1 tsp. sugar
1 tsp. cornstarch
Salt and pepper

Twintastico Italian Sausage-in-the-Hole with a Racy Red Wine Sauce

"What's golden, Italian, and big and rises every time? Our Italian sausage-in-the-hole, of course!"

Served with a racy red wine sauce, this is our Italian Twintastico Twist on the English classic "Toad-in-the-Hole."

Preheat oven to 425F.

To make Italian sausage-in-the-hole, in a large skillet over medium heat, add 1 tbsp. oil. Cook the sausages and onions for 5 minutes. Add the fennel, rosemary, and sage and cook for another 3 minutes. Turn the sausages and onions frequently until browned and onions start to caramelize. Set aside.

Sift the flour into a large mixing bowl and make a well in the center. Add the eggs, milk, salt, and pepper to the well. Whisk all together to make a smooth batter.

Pour the remaining 4 tbsp. oil into a medium-sized, shallow baking dish (round, square, or rectangular). Place on the center rack of the oven for 10 minutes, to allow the oil to become very hot.

Remove the dish from the oven, and add all the ingredients from the pan with the sausages into the hot oil. Pour over the batter. You should hear it sizzle; this is the sound you want to hear. Bake for 25-30 minutes until puffed up and golden.

To make the sauce, in a medium saucepan over high heat, sauté the shallots in a little oil for about 3 minutes, until lightly browned. Add the rosemary. Cook for 2 more minutes, stirring often.

Pour in the balsamic vinegar and cook until reduced to a syrup. Then pour in the wine and cook until reduced by two-thirds, about 15 minutes. Pour in the stock and bring to a boil.

Reduce the heat and add the sugar. Simmer until reduced by two-thirds again, about 20 minutes (stir occasionally). Using a sieve, strain the liquid over a bowl to remove all bits, and discard the bits. Then return the sauce to the saucepan over low heat.

In a small bowl, add the cornstarch to a little water and mix well. Add this to the sauce and whisk for 1 minute, until the sauce has thickened. Season with salt and pepper. Pour generously over our Italian Sausage-in-the-Hole.

Serves 6

Italian Bangers and Mash

"Everyone loves a pair of bangers!"

Bangers and mash, also known as sausages and mash, is a traditional dish in Britain. Mashed potatoes and sausages in a thick onion gravy go perfectly together. This is our Italian version of the British classic. The tomato paste gives the mash a vibrant color and elevates the flavor.

BANGERS

4 Italian sausages
1 red onion, sliced
1 tbsp. all-purpose flour
2 tbsp. balsamic vinegar
1 sprig fresh thyme
Splash Worcestershire sauce
2½ oz. marsala wine
1 cup beef stock
Salt and pepper

ITALIAN MASH

1 lb. potatoes, peeled and cut into even dice
2 garlic cloves, finely chopped
1 tbsp. tomato paste
½ stick butter
1 cup grated Parmigiano Reggiano
2 tbsp. chopped flat-leaf parsley
Drizzle of extra-virgin olive oil
Salt and pepper

In a skillet over medium heat, cook sausages for 10 minutes or until browned. Add the onions and cook for another 5 minutes. Add the flour and balsamic vinegar, and continue cooking for about 5 minutes. Add thyme and Worcestershire sauce, then gradually add marsala wine and stock. Bring to a boil, then simmer for 5 minutes and season with salt and pepper.

Cook the potatoes in boiling salted water until tender. Drain the potatoes and place in a bowl. Add the garlic, tomato paste, butter, Parmigiano Reggiano, flat-leaf parsley, and extra-virgin olive oil. Season with salt and pepper and mash together until a smooth consistency.

Serve the sausages and onion gravy alongside the Italian mash and enjoy.

Serves 2

Sassy Stromboli

Stromboli is a bit like a rolled-up pizza. Since making stromboli is very easy and fun, it's a great way to get your kids in the kitchen and cook together as a family. The best part is that you can fill it with whatever ingredients you fancy.

PIZZA DOUGH

5 cups all-purpose or bread flour
1 cup water
2¼ tsp. fast-acting dry yeast
2 tsp. salt
1 tsp. sugar
2 tbsp. extra-virgin olive oil

FILLING

2 cups tomato puree
1 cup grated Parmigiano Reggiano
2 garlic cloves, finely chopped
10 slices salami
5 slices prosciutto di Parma
5 slices mortadella
1 cup sliced fresh mozzarella
Fresh basil leaves
Salt and pepper

For the pizza dough, combine all the ingredients in a large bowl. Turn the dough out onto a floured work surface and knead for about 5 minutes until a smooth ball. Place the dough in a large oiled bowl, drizzle extra-virgin olive oil over the dough, and rub in. Cover with plastic wrap and allow to rise for about 2 hours or until doubled in size.

Roll out the dough on a lightly floured surface into a rectangle measuring about 17x13 inches.

Spread the tomato puree over the dough, leaving a 1-inch border around the edge. Then generously sprinkle the Parmigiano Reggiano and garlic over the top. Cover the sauce with a single layer of salami, prosciutto, and mortadella. Tear the mozzarella into small pieces and dot over the top, then scatter the basil leaves on top. Season with salt and pepper.

Preheat oven to 350F.

Roll the dough up into a log to enclose the filling, gently sealing the ends of the roll as you go. When you get to the end that has no filling on it, gently press to seal, then place the roll seam-side down on a nonstick baking sheet. Brush extra-virgin olive oil over the dough, and season with a little more salt and pepper. Bake in the center of the oven until golden brown and puffy, 25-30 minutes. Allow the stromboli to cool for 5 minutes before cutting it into thick slices.

Serves 6

Regina Margherita Pizza

"When the moon hits your eye like a big pizza pie, that's amore."

Pizza originated as a plain, flat bread—poor man's street food. It gradually acquired toppings, such as tomatoes in Naples in the 18th century. Regina in Italian means "queen," and in 1889, a famous Neapolitan pizza-maker, Raffaele Esposito, created a pizza for Queen Margherita using the colors of the Italian flag—tomato, mozzarella, and basil. The pizza was a hit with the queen and over time became a hit all over the world. This is how the name "Margherita pizza" was born! For us, pizza is life, and the only way to get the authentic flavor is to cook it in a traditional wood-burning pizza oven. But if you don't have one and want to make pizza at home, this is the next best thing. There are lots of different regional styles of pizza in Italy. This recipe is one of our favorites.

PIZZA DOUGH

5 cups 00 all-purpose or bread flour
2¼ tsp. fast-acting dry yeast
2 tsp. salt
1 cup water
2 tbsp. extra-virgin olive oil

TOPPING

1 cup tomato puree
Salt and pepper
Extra-virgin olive oil
¼ cup grated Parmigiano Reggiano
1 cup sliced fresh mozzarella
Fresh basil leaves

Place a pizza stone in the oven and preheat oven to 475F. If you don't have a pizza stone, you can use a large baking sheet turned upside down.

First make the dough. In a large bowl, combine flour, yeast, and salt. Gradually add the water and olive oil, mixing well until you obtain a dough. Place dough on a lightly floured work surface and knead for about 10 minutes. Cover with a damp cloth or plastic wrap and allow to rest in a warm place for about 2 hours until the dough has doubled in size.

Meanwhile, prepare the topping. Place the tomato puree in a bowl, season with salt and pepper, and drizzle in a little extra-virgin olive oil.

Once the dough has doubled in size, it's time to make the pizza. Sprinkle some flour onto a clean work surface, and with your fingers, spread the dough into a round pizza shape, or roll out using a rolling pin. Make the dough as thin as you can but be careful not to tear it. Remove the pizza stone or baking sheet from the oven, and place the pizza on it.

Spread the tomato sauce evenly over the pizza, to the edges. Sprinkle with Parmigiano Reggiano, and top with mozzarella. Drizzle a little extra-virgin olive oil over the top.

Bake for 8-10 minutes. Scatter a few fresh basil leaves over the top, and serve.

Serves 2-4

Italian Tacos

"Everyone loves a good taco, and here we put our Italian beef into those tacos!"

We love to play around with food and create new recipes. Here is our Italian Twintastico Twist on the classic taco.

Extra-virgin olive oil
1 large onion, finely chopped
5 garlic cloves, finely chopped
2 tbsp. red pepper flakes
1 lb. ground beef
2½ cups tomato puree
3 tbsp. tomato paste
10 fresh basil leaves, finely chopped
Salt and pepper
6 soft corn tortillas or corn taco shells
1 cup shredded mozzarella
Blessed Basil Pesto (see index)
2 cups mascarpone
1 small iceberg lettuce, finely sliced or chopped
1 tomato, chopped
1 cup grated Parmigiano Reggiano

In a large, heavy skillet, heat the olive oil. Add the onions, garlic, and red pepper flakes and cook until garlic is golden. Then add the ground beef and cook, stirring frequently, until meat is almost done.

Add the tomato puree, tomato paste, and basil leaves and mix well. Cook, stirring frequently, until the sauce reduces and thickens and the meat is cooked all the way through. Season with salt and pepper, reduce heat to low, and simmer for about 2 hours.

Now it's time to make your Italian Tacos. Place a generous amount of the Italian meat down the center of a tortilla or into the bottom of a taco shell. Top with shredded mozzarella, then pesto sauce, followed by a dollop of the mascarpone. Sprinkle on the chopped lettuce and tomato to add some crunch and freshness, followed by the grated Parmigiano Reggiano cheese to finish. Repeat with remaining ingredients.

Serves 4-6

Italian Yorkshire Puddings

Here is our Italian Twintastico Twist on the traditional Yorkshire pudding. A Yorkshire pudding is a baked batter, and in Britain, it is always associated with a Sunday roast. As nice as it is, we feel that it needed an Italian lift. This recipe is very easy to make and gives a richer, deeper flavor. Adding the chopped rosemary and sage really takes our Italian Yorkshire pudding to the next level. Give this a try and you will never go back to ordinary Yorkshire puddings again.

4 eggs
1 cup milk
2 cups all-purpose flour
1 handful rosemary, finely chopped
1 handful sage, finely chopped
1 tsp. salt
Vegetable or sunflower oil

In a large bowl, whisk the eggs well. Using a large bowl will incorporate more air while whisking. Then add the milk and flour, and whisk together thoroughly.

Add the rosemary and sage, and whisk together. Add the salt and mix until you have a smooth batter.

Preheat oven to 350F.

Prepare your muffin pan. Either vegetable or sunflower oil will do, as you need an oil that can handle high heat. You need ½ inch oil in each muffin cup, so here is a cool little trick for you to get exactly that. Fill the first 3 cups to the top, then gently tilt the pan so the oil pours down to the bottom molds. You will then have an equal amount of oil in each cup, exactly what you need.

Place the oiled pan in the oven for about 15 minutes. Transfer the batter to a pitcher, ready to pour into the pan. After 15 minutes, carefully remove the pan, as the oil will be piping hot. Gently pour the batter into each cup, filling to the top, and bake at 400F for 20-25 minutes until golden brown. Do not open the oven until the Yorkshire puddings are done—this is very important! Serve immediately with a thick, smooth gravy.

Makes 12

Alberti's Amazing Italian Burgerlicious Burger

Our juicy Italian burger, packed with tantalizing flavors, is perfect for summer BBQs. . . . This is the best burger you will ever put in your mouth, we promise!

BURGERS

½ lb. ground beef
½ lb. ground pork
5 garlic cloves, finely chopped
2 eggs
1 cup breadcrumbs
1 handful basil, finely chopped
1 cup grated Parmigiano Reggiano
Salt and pepper
5 slices fresh mozzarella
5 slices provolone cheese
10 slices pancetta
5 ciabatta rolls
Extra-virgin olive oil
1 red onion, sliced
1 cup ketchup
5 whole leaves crunchy little gem lettuce (or romaine)

GARLIC MAYONNAISE

¾ cup mayonnaise
3 garlic cloves, finely chopped

In a large bowl, mix the ground beef and pork, garlic, eggs, breadcrumbs, basil, and Parmigiano Reggiano. Season with salt and pepper. Shape into burgers, then chill for at least 1 hour before you cook them. This will help them keep their shape when they're cooking.

Place the burgers on a hot griddle pan and cook for about 5 minutes, pressing down with a spatula. Turn the burgers over, top each with 1 slice mozzarella and 1 slice provolone, and continue to cook for 4-5 minutes until done. Add the pancetta to the griddle and cook until crisp.

When the burgers are cooked, cut the ciabatta rolls in half. Drizzle a little extra-virgin olive oil on each half and place cut-side down on the hot griddle until browned. Mix the garlic mayonnaise ingredients.

Now it's time to start assembling each burger. Add a nice dollop of the garlic mayonnaise to the bottom of a ciabatta roll, then place a burger on top. Add sliced red onion, 2 slices pancetta, and ketchup. Finish with a lettuce leaf and garlic mayonnaise, then top with the other half of the ciabatta roll. Repeat with remaining ingredients.

Serves 5

Italian Shepherd's Pie

This is one of Britain's favorite dishes. Here is our Italian Twintastico Twist: adding rosemary to the ground lamb gives it that extra deep flavor it needs. And instead of using mashed potatoes for the topping, we use polenta. It gives a creamier texture and works perfectly in this dish.

Extra-virgin olive oil
1 large onion, finely chopped
2-3 carrots, peeled and finely chopped
1½ lb. ground lamb
2 tbsp. tomato paste
Generous splash Worcestershire sauce
Salt and pepper
1 cup vegetable stock
Rosemary, finely chopped
8 cups water
2½ cups polenta
1½ cups grated Parmigiano Reggiano
2 sticks butter

In a skillet over high heat, add the oil. Cook the chopped onions and carrots for a few minutes, then add the ground lamb. When browned, add the tomato paste, Worcestershire sauce, salt, and pepper. Cook for a few more minutes, then add the stock and chopped rosemary. Bring to a simmer, reduce heat, and cook for about 30 minutes.

In a large saucepan, bring the water to a boil. Add the polenta gradually, whisking constantly. Reduce the heat to low and cook, stirring occasionally. After a few minutes, add the Parmigiano Reggiano, butter, salt, and pepper, and stir to combine. You want a nice smooth, thick, mash consistency.

Preheat oven to 350F.

Now pour the meat mixture into a baking dish, then cover the whole surface with the polenta. With a wooden spoon, smooth the polenta out to the edges and flatten. Ruffle the polenta with a fork to give it a fancy finish.

Bake for about 30 minutes until the polenta has browned slightly and the meat mixture is bubbling. Serve hot and generously.

Serves 6

Porky Porchetta

This is a traditional Italian savory moist boneless pork roast. The deboned suckling pig is spread out and covered with stuffing, then rolled and roasted on a spit over wood. Porchetta is usually heavily salted in addition to being stuffed with garlic, fennel, rosemary, and other herbs, often wild. Instead of suckling pig, our recipe uses pork belly for a similar effect, but nothing beats the real thing, so when in Italy, you have to try it!

11 lb. whole pork belly, deboned*
Coarse sea salt and freshly ground pepper
2 tbsp. dried thyme
2 tbsp. coarsely chopped fresh rosemary
2 tbsp. coarsely chopped fresh sage leaves
1 tbsp. fennel seeds
8 garlic cloves, finely chopped
Extra-virgin olive oil

Preheat oven to 400F. Lay the pork belly flat on a work surface, skin-side down. Sprinkle meat with 4 tbsp. salt and lots of pepper, rubbing it in well with your hands. Allow to rest for 10 minutes.

Sprinkle the herbs, fennel seeds, and garlic over the pork. Next tie up the meat. You will need 10 pieces of string, each about 1 foot long. Carefully roll up the meat crosswise, then tie very tightly with string in the middle of the roll. Tie at either end, about ½ inch in, then keep tying at intervals along the roll until all the lengths of string have been used. If any filling escapes, push it back in. Massage extra-virgin olive oil all over the roll, then rub in some salt and pepper.

Grease a large roasting pan with olive oil, then add the pork, seam-side up. Roast for 15 minutes. Turn the pork and cook, seam-side down, for another 15 minutes.

Turn the oven down to 300F and cover the pork with foil. Roast for 3 hours. Remove the pork and allow to rest for 5 minutes. Then slice and serve hot or at room temperature. Serve with roast potatoes and vegetables or, as we like to do, make a porchetta sandwich and enjoy.

*Ask your butcher to debone the meat, score the skin well, and trim off excess fat. The trimmed weight should be about 6½ lb.

Serves 8

Dolci

A great meal always ends with a great dessert, and Italians do them the best. After dessert comes the coffee, which in Italy means an espresso. Coffee for us is life. It is usually followed by limoncello, grappa, sambuca, or even a caffè corretto, which is a shot of espresso with a small amount of liquor. *La dolce vita.*

We like our coffee like we like our women . . . Italian, strong, and keeps us up all night.

Twillionaire's Shortbread

Here is our take on the classic Millionaire's Shortbread . . . Twinning Style. An indulgent treat with a crisp cookie base, soft caramel center, and topping of chocolate with crunchy amaretti cookie pieces, our Twillionaire's Shortbread is the best. The texture and almond flavor of the amaretti take this recipe to another level.

SHORTBREAD

1½ cups all-purpose flour
3 sticks cold unsalted butter, cut into cubes
1 cup superfine sugar

TOPPING

3 sticks butter
1½ cups condensed milk
1 cup dark corn syrup
1 cup dark chocolate chips
4 cups Nutella
Crushed amaretti cookies

Preheat oven to 300F. Grease and line a 9-inch square baking dish with parchment paper. In a food processor, pulse the flour and butter cubes until the mixture resembles fine breadcrumbs. (Alternatively, you can rub in the butter by hand.)

Add the sugar and pulse again until combined. Tip the mixture into the lined baking dish and spread it out evenly with the back of a spoon. Then press the shortbread down firmly with your knuckles or the back of a spoon, so that it is tightly packed in the dish. Bake for 30 minutes or until very light golden brown. Set aside to cool.

Meanwhile, for the topping, heat the butter, condensed milk, and syrup in a saucepan, stirring occasionally until the butter is melted and the mixture is smooth. Increase the heat and bring the mixture to a boil, stirring frequently. The caramel will thicken and turn golden brown. Set aside to cool slightly, then pour over the cooled shortbread. Allow to cool completely.

In the top of a double boiler, melt the chocolate chips and Nutella over simmering water (ensure that the bottom of the bowl does not touch the water). Stir occasionally. Pour the melted chocolate over the caramel, then sprinkle on the crushed amaretti while chocolate is still warm. Put in the fridge for 30 minutes until set completely. Cut into squares and serve.

Serves about 10

Torta di Limoncello

When life gives you lemons . . . make a limoncello cake! Fresh and vibrant, with lots of zest, it's perfect for a summer's day.

CAKE

1 cup mascarpone
2 eggs
⅓ cup extra-virgin olive oil
2 tbsp. lemon juice
1 tbsp. lemon zest
1 cup superfine sugar
2 oz. limoncello liqueur
2 cups all-purpose flour
1 tsp. baking powder
Pinch of salt

ICING

1 cup powdered sugar
2 oz. limoncello liqueur
Lemon peels

Preheat oven to 350F. Grease a 9-inch cake pan or line with parchment paper.

In a large bowl, whisk together the mascarpone, eggs, olive oil, lemon juice, lemon zest, sugar, and limoncello. In a separate bowl, mix the flour, baking powder, and salt. Gently stir the dry ingredients into the wet. Do not overmix, or the cake will be tough. Pour cake mixture into prepared pan.

Bake until top is golden and a skewer inserted in the center of the cake comes out clean, about 35 minutes. Remove from oven and allow to cool slightly. Then remove cake from pan.

In a small bowl, stir the powdered sugar and limoncello together until smooth. Spoon the icing over the cake and spread with the back of a spoon. The icing will seep into the cake and add moisture. Decorate the top with lemon peels.

Serves 8

Cheeky Chestnut Cake

Originally from Tuscany, this recipe is a favorite of our Nonna's. It always puts a smile on her face when we make it for her. We remember her telling us stories of how she would grind the chestnuts to make this cake on the farm in Italy when she was young, and this is our version of the recipe in honor of her.

1¼ cups chestnut flour
1 cup brown sugar
4 eggs
1 stick butter, softened
1 tbsp. cocoa powder
1 tsp. baking powder
1 tsp. vanilla extract
⅔ cup dark chocolate chips
Mascarpone
Cocoa powder or powdered sugar for garnish

Preheat oven to 325F. Grease a 9-inch springform pan with a little oil or butter, and line the base with parchment paper.

Sift the chestnut flour into a large bowl. Add the sugar, eggs, butter, cocoa powder, baking powder, and vanilla extract. Using an electric hand mixer, whisk until smooth. Fold in the chocolate chips.

Pour the mixture into the prepared pan. Bake for 35 minutes or until risen and the sides pull away from the pan. Remove from oven and allow to cool.

Using a small metal spatula, loosen the sides of the cake from the pan, and spring it out of the pan. To serve, add a dollop of mascarpone and sprinkle with cocoa powder or powdered sugar.

Serves 8

Torta di Nocciole

Hazelnuts are the real star of the show in this cake from Italy's Piedmont region. The frangelico liqueur brings out the hazelnut flavor. Along with the moist center, it really will drive you nutty!

3 eggs
1½ cups superfine sugar
½ cup extra-virgin olive oil
½ cup whole milk
1 tsp. vanilla extract
2 oz. frangelico liqueur
2 cups all-purpose flour
1 tsp. baking powder
1 cup ground hazelnuts
Powdered sugar
Whipped cream or Nutella

Preheat oven to 350F degrees. Grease an 8-inch springform pan, and line the base with parchment paper. In a bowl, beat the eggs. Add the sugar, olive oil, milk, vanilla extract, and frangelico. Mix well until smooth.

Stir in the flour, baking powder, and ground hazelnuts. Mix well until smooth. Pour the mixture into the prepared pan.

Bake for 45 minutes. Remove from oven, and just before serving, remove from pan and dust top with powdered sugar. Serve with whipped cream, or our favorite, Nutella. We obviously prefer Nutella with everything, so we would go with that!

Serves 8

Extra-virgin olive oil
½ cup good-quality cocoa powder, sifted
½ cup hot water
2 tsp. vanilla extract
1 cup ground hazelnuts
1 tsp. baking powder
2 cups superfine sugar
3 large eggs
Powdered sugar
Vanilla ice cream, vanilla gelato, or mascarpone
Crushed amaretti cookies

Olive Oil Cake

This dense chocolate cake is rich with a moist center and has the added health benefits of extra-virgin olive oil. As we all know, olive oil is the cornerstone of the Mediterranean diet—a nutritional mainstay of the world's oldest cultures. But don't worry, the olive oil is only just detectable and gives a silky-smooth texture. For us, olive oil is like liquid gold, and we use it every day. Our favorite Italian beauty, Sophia Loren, was stunning in her 1960s heyday, and she still is now. Her secret? Extra-virgin olive oil. Sophia's Mediterranean diet includes olive oil every day, and she routinely rubs a small amount into her skin, which keeps her complexion lustrous and moisturized. She even adds a few capfuls into a hot bath for a nourishing skin soak! We love Sophia Loren, and if it's good enough for her, it's good enough for us.

Preheat oven to 325F. Grease a 9-inch springform pan with a little oil, and line the base with parchment paper.

In a bowl, measure and sift the cocoa powder. Whisk in the hot water until you have a smooth, chocolatey, still-runny paste. Whisk in the vanilla extract, then set aside to cool a little.

In a small bowl, combine the ground hazelnuts and baking powder. In a large bowl, add the sugar, ½ cup olive oil, and eggs, and whisk together until you have a pale, thickened cream. Or use a stand mixer with the paddle attachment, and beat together vigorously for about 3 minutes until you have a pale, thickened cream.

Add the cocoa mixture to the egg mixture, and whisk until well combined. Add the ground hazelnut mixture and combine. If using a mixer, reduce the speed a little and pour in the cocoa mixture, beating as you go. When all is scraped down in the mixer, slowly add the ground hazelnut mixture.

Scrape down, stir a little with a spatula, then pour the batter into the prepared pan. Bake for 40-45 minutes or until the sides are set and the very center on top still looks slightly moist. A cake tester should come out with a few sticky crumbs attached.

Let cake cool for 10 minutes on a wire rack, still in its pan. Then, using a small metal spatula, loosen the sides of the cake from the pan, and spring it out of the pan. Allow to cool completely, or serve while still warm. Dust powdered sugar over the top. Serve with a scoop of vanilla ice cream, vanilla gelato, or mascarpone on the side with crushed amaretti on top of the ice cream, gelato, or mascarpone.

Serves 6

Luscious Lemon Ricotta Cake

Ricotta keeps this cake light, fluffy, and moist. It has just enough lemon to add that extra zesty zing.

3 eggs
1½ cups superfine sugar
5 tbsp. extra-virgin olive oil
1 cup whole-milk ricotta, well drained
2 cups all-purpose flour
¾ cup ground almonds
1 tsp. baking powder
Zest of 2 lemons
Juice of 1 lemon
1 tsp. vanilla extract
1 tbsp. amaretto liqueur
Powdered sugar
Mascarpone, vanilla ice cream, or vanilla gelato

Preheat oven to 350F. Butter and flour a cake pan.

In a large bowl, beat the eggs with the sugar until pale and creamy. Add the olive oil and ricotta, and mix until smooth. Gently fold in the flour, ground almonds, and baking powder, then add the lemon zest and juice, vanilla extract, and amaretto.

Pour the batter into the prepared pan. Bake for 35-40 minutes or until a skewer inserted into the middle comes out clean. Allow to cool completely for up to 30 minutes in the pan before turning out onto a plate.

Dust with powdered sugar and serve with a scoop of mascarpone, vanilla ice cream, or vanilla gelato.

Serves 6

Torta Caprese

This gloriously rich chocolate cake with ground nuts hails from Capri. It beautifully reflects that island's simplicity and elegance. Serve a slice with a glass of Vin Santo.

6 oz. fine-quality bittersweet chocolate (not unsweetened)
1¾ sticks unsalted butter
4 large eggs
1 cup granulated sugar
Pinch of salt
1¼ cups ground almonds
Powdered sugar
Mascarpone

Preheat oven to 350F. Butter a 10-inch cake pan.

Break the chocolate into the top of a double boiler and add the butter. Place over a saucepan of gently simmering water. Heat gently until just melted (do not stir), then remove the pan from the heat and stir. Then separate the eggs. In a bowl, whisk yolks with sugar until very thick and pale.

In another bowl, whisk the egg whites with a pinch of salt until they just hold stiff peaks. Pour the melted chocolate into the bowl with the egg yolks and sugar, and mix thoroughly. Stir in ground almonds. Using a metal spoon, gently fold one-third of the egg whites into the mixture. Fold in the remaining egg whites in 2 stages.

Pour the mixture into the prepared cake pan and spread it out evenly. Bake in the center of the oven for 50 minutes, or until the sides begin to pull away from the pan. Cool on a rack for 5 minutes before turning out onto a plate. Dust with powdered sugar and serve with a scoop of mascarpone.

Serves 8

Perfetto Polenta Cake

This beautiful cake is perfect to enjoy for dessert or in the afternoon with a cup of coffee or tea. It's very moist and light, with a sticky orange syrup, just the way we like it. Serve it with a scoop of mascarpone, vanilla ice cream, or vanilla gelato on the side that is topped with crushed amaretti cookies for texture.

CAKE

3 eggs
1¼ cups superfine sugar
Zest and juice of 2 oranges
⅔ cup polenta
1½ cups ground almonds
1 tsp. baking powder

ORANGE SYRUP

1 cup superfine sugar
Juice of 3 oranges
2½ oz. Aperol liqueur

Preheat oven to 350F. Butter the base of a 9-inch springform pan and line with parchment paper.

In a large bowl, whisk the eggs and sugar until the sugar has dissolved and the eggs are pale in color. Fold in the orange zest and juice. Then add the polenta, ground almonds, and baking powder, and mix together.

Pour the mixture into the pan and spread evenly. Bake for 40-45 minutes. Cool in the pan and set aside.

To prepare the syrup, in a saucepan, heat the sugar slowly until the sugar melts and caramel-colored bubbles appear. Pour in the orange juice and Aperol, and bring to a boil. Cook for 5-10 minutes or until the liquid has reduced by half.

Remove the cooled cake from the pan and place on a serving plate. Drizzle the syrup over the cake and around the plate.

Serves 6

CRUST

3 cups all-purpose flour
¾ cup superfine sugar
Zest of 1 lemon
Pinch of salt
1½ sticks unsalted butter, cut into pieces
1 tsp. vanilla extract
2 eggs
1 egg yolk

FILLING AND TOPPING

4 cups milk
Peel of ½ lemon (in 1 piece)
6 egg yolks
½ cup all-purpose flour
1 cup superfine sugar
1 tsp. vanilla extract
½ cup pine nuts
Powdered sugar

Torta della Nonna

A classic, Tuscan-born tart, **Torta della Nonna** *has to be one of the most well known Italian desserts. Its success likely lies in its simplicity: it consists of nothing more than a double-crusted tart enclosing a creamy heart of lemon-scented custard. The top is studded with crunchy pine nuts and dusted with powdered sugar.*

To prepare the crusts, in a food processor, add the flour, sugar, lemon zest, salt, and butter. Pulse until the mixture resembles a coarse meal. Add the vanilla extract, eggs, and egg yolk, and mix just until the dough comes together. Collect the dough and divide into 2 pieces, a large and a smaller piece (about ⅔ and ⅓ of the dough). Pat into 2 discs, wrap each separately in plastic wrap, and refrigerate for about 1 hour.

To prepare the custard filling, in a pan, heat the milk with the lemon peel until hot but not boiling. In a separate saucepan, add the egg yolks, flour, sugar, and vanilla extract. Whisk well until light and fluffy.

To the egg mixture, add a little bit of the hot milk (discarding the lemon peel), and whisk some more. Incorporate the rest of the milk while whisking. Place the pan over medium heat and bring to a slow boil, stirring. The custard will thicken, so make sure it doesn't stick to the bottom.

When the custard starts to bubble, reduce the heat and cook for 1 or 2 more minutes, until it reaches the desired thickness. Pour the custard in a glass bowl, and place plastic wrap directly on the custard, to prevent a skin from forming. Set aside to cool.

Preheat oven to 350F.

Butter and flour an 11-inch tart pan. On a lightly floured surface, roll out the larger disc of dough to a circle about 12 inches in diameter. Roll the circle loosely over the rolling pin, and move the dough to the tart pan. If the dough breaks, you can easily fix it with your fingers, so don't worry! Carefully arrange the circle across the bottom and up the sides of the pan. Trim any excess dough that comes above the edges of the pan, or add little pieces if needed. Prick the bottom with a fork.

Pour the custard cream over the dough in the tart pan, and spread. Roll out the other disc to a circle about 11 inches in diameter, and place it on top of the custard. You need to be a little more careful this time.

Trim any excess dough from the edges, and press the edges of the top and bottom crusts together to seal. Gently prick the top with a fork just a little. Brush the top with some milk. Top the tart with pine nuts, and press them down gently so they adhere to the crust. Bake in lower third of the oven for about 45 minutes, until slightly golden on top and around the edges.

Allow to cool at room temperature, then chill in the refrigerator for 1 hour before removing from the pan, dusting with powdered sugar, and cutting your first slice . . . for yourself, of course!

Serves 10-12

Italian Almond Cheesecake

Who doesn't love cheesecake? This baked cheesecake is a perfect dessert for entertaining. And it's Italian—what more could you want?

2 cups crushed amaretti cookies
½ stick unsalted butter, melted
Seeds from 1 vanilla bean, or 2 tsp. vanilla extract
2 cups ricotta
1 cup superfine sugar
3 large eggs
1 cup mascarpone
1 cup ground almonds
1 tsp. baking powder
2 tbsp. cornstarch
Zest of 1 lemon
1 cup sliced almonds
Powdered sugar
Whipped cream

Preheat oven to 350F. In a large bowl, add the crushed cookies. Pour over the melted butter, and mix well.

Pour the crumb mixture into the base of an 8-inch nonstick springform pan, and press down firmly with the back of a spoon. Chill in the fridge for 5-10 minutes.

Meanwhile, in a large bowl, add the vanilla seeds, ricotta, sugar, eggs, mascarpone, ground almonds, baking powder, cornstarch, and lemon zest. Using an electric hand mixer, beat until smooth. Pour into the prepared pan and scatter on the sliced almonds.

Place on a baking sheet and bake for 45 minutes until golden. It may feel a little wobbly, but it will set as it cools. Turn off the oven, open the door, and leave the cheesecake inside until completely cool. Chill in the fridge for another hour or more. Dust with powdered sugar and serve with whipped cream.

Serves 8

Nutty Nutella Cheesecake

Money can't buy happiness, but it can buy Nutella, and that is basically the same thing! This nutty, chocolatey, indulgent cheesecake is very, very naughty. It is so easy to make, rich in flavor, surprisingly light, and even better . . . it's no bake!

36 Oreo, chocolate chip, or hazelnut cookies
1 stick unsalted butter, softened
2 cups mascarpone, room temperature
½ cup powdered sugar
2 cups Nutella, room temperature
¾ cup coarsely chopped hazelnuts

Break the cookies into the bowl of a food processor. Add the butter and process until the mixture starts to clump. Tip into a 9-inch springform pan, and press into the base with your hands or the back of a spoon. Chill in the fridge for 30 minutes.

In a large bowl, beat the mascarpone and powdered sugar until smooth. Add the Nutella and continue beating until combined and smooth.

Carefully smooth the Nutella mixture over the cookie base. Cover with chopped hazelnuts, and chill in the fridge for at least 2 hours or overnight. Using a small metal spatula, loosen the sides of the cake from the pan, and spring it out of the pan. Serve straight from the fridge for best results.

Serves 8

Our Big and Bouncy Bomboloni Italian Balls

Bomboloni are Italian doughnuts, and they are as much fun to say as they are to make and eat. They are like a party in your mouth, with their gooey centers and sugary, soft dough. They are delightful even without a filling, but if you fill them with Nutella, jam, or pastry cream, you will be more than satisfied, that's for sure!

3 cups bread or all-purpose flour
2¼ tsp. fast-acting dry yeast
2 tsp. salt
¼ cup granulated sugar
Zest of 1 lemon
2 eggs, lightly beaten
¾ cup whole milk
½ stick cup butter, cubed
1 tsp. vanilla extract
Vegetable oil
Granulated sugar for coating
Nutella, jam, or pastry cream

In a large bowl, or the bowl of a stand mixer fitted with a dough hook, combine the flour, yeast, salt, sugar, and lemon zest. In a separate bowl, whisk the eggs with the milk. Add the butter and vanilla extract, and mix well. Pour the wet ingredients into the dry ingredients. Knead the dough in the stand mixer for 2 minutes, or if making the dough by hand, tip it onto a floured work surface and knead for about 5 minutes, until it's smooth and elastic but still quite sticky.

Transfer the dough to a large, lightly oiled bowl. Cover with plastic wrap and allow to rise in a warm place for 1 hour or until doubled in size.

Using a rolling pin, roll out the dough until about ¾ inch thick. Then, using a round pastry cutter the size of a cup, cut the dough into disks. Place the dough on a baking sheet lined with parchment paper, and cover with plastic wrap. Allow to rise for another hour.

Heat oil in a large, deep pan to 350F. Fry the doughnuts, in batches, for 4-5 minutes, turning halfway through the cooking time, until golden brown. Remove with a slotted spoon and drain on paper towels.

Dredge the doughnuts in granulated sugar until completely covered. Spoon the filling of your choice—Nutella, jam, or pastry cream—into a piping bag with a medium nozzle. Make a small hole in the side of each doughnut, push in the nozzle, and squeeze to fill the bomboloni. Serve warm.

Serves about 10

Alberti's Amazing Almond Muffins

Everyone loves sweet, moist muffins. They smell and taste amazing and are quick and easy to make.

2 cups all-purpose flour
1 cup ground almonds
2 tsp. baking powder
½ tsp. salt
1½ cups white chocolate chips
⅓ cup melted butter
2 oz. frangelico liqueur
2 tsp. vanilla extract
1¼ cups whole milk
2 eggs
1 cup granulated sugar
½ cup sliced almonds

Preheat oven to 375F. Prepare a muffin pan with nonstick cooking spray or paper liners and set aside.

In a large bowl, combine the flour, ground almonds, baking powder, and salt. Add chocolate chips, give it all a big stir, and set aside.

In a separate bowl, whisk together the butter, frangelico liqueur, vanilla extract, milk, eggs, and sugar. Pour into the dry ingredients and mix everything together.

Using an ice-cream scoop, divide your batter evenly among the muffin pans. Top with a few sliced almonds and pop them in the oven to bake for about 20 minutes. Remove and let cool. Then dig in!

Makes about 15

Alberti's Nutcracker

"Everyone loves our Italian nuts!"

This recipe for Italian almond brittle brings back very fond memories of spending summers in Italy growing up. We used to have this around festival times, from carnivals to Christmas. Actually it is found year round all over Italy, most often at street fairs, where stalls bearing all sorts of traditional treats sell hefty blocks wrapped in cellophane. You can use any sort of nuts: hazelnuts, peanuts, pistachios, almonds, or even a mixture. Sticky, chewy, and crunchy—this brittle is a real treat for the whole family . . . but watch those teeth!

1 cup granulated sugar
1¼ cups almonds
1 lemon, halved

In a saucepan over high heat, cook the sugar. Stir until the sugar begins to liquefy and turns golden in color. Continue to cook until the sugar turns golden brown and becomes a beautiful sticky liquid, 4-5 minutes.

Remove from heat, add the almonds, and mix well to fully coat. Quickly pour and spread the hot almond-sugar mixture onto a sheet of parchment paper. Place another sheet of parchment face down on top of the almond mixture. Using a rolling pin on top of the parchment, roll mixture flat, about ½ inch thick, or you can spread it out, without parchment on top, using an oiled metal spatula. Once flat, peel off the parchment paper and rub half a lemon over the nut brittle to give it a citrus flavor and a shine.

Allow to cool for 15 minutes, then break into small pieces or cut into strips.

Serves about 10

Panna Cotta con Frutti di Bosco

This delicious dessert, our Mamma's favorite, is made simply with cream cooked on the stove, then thickened up with gelatin and flavored with vanilla and sugar. No milk is used in a traditional panna cotta. You know it's a good panna cotta when you shake the plate and the panna cotta wobbles. We love things that wobble! Frutti di bosco is Italian for "fruits of the forest," or mixed berries. This is our favorite flavor with panna cotta, but you can use any fruit or sauce you like. If you don't want to use fruit, panna cotta is also good with caramel or chocolate sauce poured on top. Don't worry about calories. As we always say, everything in moderation, including moderation!

PANNA COTTA

3 gelatin sheets
2 cups heavy cream
¾ cup superfine sugar
Seeds from 1 vanilla bean, or 1 tbsp. vanilla extract

FRUTTI DI BOSCO

1 cup mixed berries
½ cup superfine sugar

For the panna cotta, add the gelatin sheets to a bowl of cold water and allow to soak until soft, about 10 minutes. In a large pan, add the cream, sugar, and vanilla and bring to a simmer. Remove from heat.

Squeeze excess water from the gelatin sheets, and add gelatin to the pan. Using a whisk, mix well until gelatin has fully dissolved in the cream. Pour into ramekins or dariole molds and allow to cool. Refrigerate until set, at least 2 hours but preferably overnight.

To unmold, dip the base of each mold into warm water for a few seconds, then turn panna cotta out onto small serving plates.

For the topping, add the mixed berries and sugar to a pan and boil for about 5 minutes. Allow to cool, then refrigerate. Serve the chilled sauce over the panna cotta. You can add as much or little as you want. We always like a lot.

Serves 4

Babbo's Biscotti

Babbo means "Daddy" in Tuscan dialect. These are our Papà's favorite, and we always make an espresso for him to dunk them in. Biscotti literally means "twice cooked" in Italian, and the double baking makes it twice as nice. These crunchy, sweet Italian treats date back to the 13th century. The dough is baked in a log, then sliced and baked again so the cookies dry and crisp up, hence the name biscotti. There are many different ways to flavor your biscotti. They are delicious with tea or coffee, but you can also enjoy them the traditional Italian way, dipped into Vin Santo or a sweet wine.

2 cups all-purpose flour
Pinch of salt
1 tsp. baking powder
1 cup superfine sugar
2 large eggs
1 tsp. vanilla extract
1½ cups whole almonds, coarsely chopped

Preheat oven to 350F. In a bowl, mix the flour, pinch of salt, and baking powder. The salt will enhance the other flavors.

In another bowl, using an electric hand mixer, beat the sugar, eggs, and vanilla until pale yellow, about 3 minutes. Stir the beaten eggs and sugar into the dry mixture, a little at a time, making sure each addition is incorporated before adding the next. Then add the almonds and mix well until you have a firm dough. The dough shouldn't be sticky at all.

Turn the biscotti dough out onto a floured surface, then divide in half.

Roll the dough into 2 logs, each about 14 inches long and 3-4 inches wide. Line a baking sheet with parchment paper, and transfer logs to the sheet. Bake for 30-40 minutes. Remove from oven and cool on a wire rack for 10 minutes. Transfer to a board and cut the logs into 1-inch-thick slices.

Place the slices back on the baking sheet, and bake for another 15-20 minutes, or until the biscotti are dry through to the center. Transfer to a wire rack and allow to cool completely until ready to serve.

Makes about 30

Romantic Ricotta Balls

"Baci, baci . . . kiss, kiss."

Our Romantic Ricotta Balls are a hot, soft, melt-in-the-mouth, sexy dessert. Set them out mounded on a dish, accompanied by coffee, and watch them fly off the table.

1 cup ricotta
2 large eggs
¾ cup all-purpose flour
1 tsp. baking powder
Pinch of salt
½ tsp. cinnamon
1 tbsp. superfine sugar
1 tsp. vanilla extract
Vegetable oil
Powdered sugar

In a large bowl, combine ricotta and eggs, and mix until smooth. Add flour, baking powder, salt, cinnamon, sugar, and vanilla. Mix again to make a smooth batter.

Fill a wide, deep skillet with about 1 inch oil. Heat over medium-high heat until a bit of batter sizzles when dropped in. Using a spoon or ice-cream scoop, drop rounded teaspoons of batter into the pan, 5 or 6 at a time. After about 1 minute, when the batter puffs up and the undersides turn golden brown, flip the balls and allow to brown again for about 1 more minute. Transfer the balls to paper towels, just to remove the excess oil, and continue frying until all batter is used.

Pile the ricotta balls in a pyramid shape on a serving plate. Using a sieve, sprinkle powdered sugar evenly and generously over the ricotta balls. Serve immediately.

Makes about 20

Naughty Nutella Pancakes

We love pancakes. Who doesn't? Our light and fluffy Naughty Nutella Pancakes are the best. You will have lots of fun making them with the whole family. Flipping the pancakes is the best part—it's all in the wrist! These are so flipping good, you will go back for more and more.

PANCAKES

1¼ cups all-purpose flour
1 tsp. baking powder
2 tbsp. superfine sugar
⅔ cup milk
1 large egg
Butter

TOPPING

1 cup Nutella
Hazelnuts, coarsely chopped
Strawberries
Whipped cream or mascarpone
Maple syrup, optional

In a large bowl, whisk all pancake ingredients, except butter, until smooth. The mixture shouldn't be too runny, with a consistency of thick cream.

In a hot skillet, melt a little butter. Pour in enough pancake batter to make 1 pancake of your desired thickness, making sure it spreads around the pan evenly. Wait until the top of the pancake begins to bubble, then flip it over and cook until both sides are golden. Remove the pancake and repeat until all the batter is used.

Once you're ready to serve, spread each pancake with a generous amount of Nutella, then stack them so you have a layer of Nutella between each pancake.

Sprinkle hazelnuts over the stack, and serve with a side of fresh strawberries and whipped cream or mascarpone. This is indulgence at its best. If you want to be really naughty, which we are, drizzle a generous amount of maple syrup on top!

Serves 4

CANNOLI SHELLS

2 cups all-purpose flour
2 tbsp. unsalted butter or shortening
3 tsp. superfine sugar
½ tsp. cinnamon
1 egg, separated
¾ cup marsala or Italian white wine
Vegetable oil

FILLING

3 cups whole-milk ricotta
1½ cups powdered sugar
Zest of 1 lemon
1 tsp. vanilla extract
Cocoa powder or powdered sugar for dusting
Chopped pistachios, mini chocolate chips, or
candied fruit, optional

The Big Cannoli

"Leave the gun; take the cannoli."

Everyone loves our big Italian cannoli. Cannoli are basically crisp, sweet tubes with a ricotta filling. They are a very popular treat in Sicily. This is a traditional recipe for cannoli using ricotta. You will need 3 to 4 metal cannoli tubes, which are available at most kitchen stores. Do not fill the cannoli too far in advance, or they may become soggy. To finish your cannoli, you can decorate the ends with chopped pistachios, mini chocolate chips, or candied fruit.

In a bowl, sift the flour. Add the butter, and using your fingertips, rub it into the flour until the consistency of fine crumbs. Stir in the sugar and cinnamon. Make a well in the center of the flour, and add the egg yolk to the well. Using a wooden spoon, start to draw the flour into the egg, and mix together.

Add the wine gradually and continue mixing until you have a smooth dough. Use your fingers to bring the dough together. Turn it out onto a well-floured surface.

Knead the dough for 5 minutes until smooth, and form into a ball. Wrap in plastic wrap and allow to rest for 10 minutes. Then lightly flour a work surface and roll the dough out into a thin circle, about ⅛ inch thick. Using a 3½- to 4-inch round cookie cutter, cut out as many circles as possible, then gather the scraps, reroll, and cut out more.

Fill a large saucepan two-thirds full with oil. Heat gently until a small piece of the cannoli dough sizzles, rises to the surface, and browns within 1 minute.

Wrap the dough circles carefully around the cannoli tubes, and seal the closures with a dab of egg white. Lower the cannoli into the oil 3-4 at a time, and cook for 1-2 minutes, turning once, until crisp and golden. Remove from the oil with a slotted spoon and drain on paper towels; set aside until cooled. Remove the cannoli from the tubes, and repeat with the remaining circles.

To make the filling, in a bowl, mix the ricotta, powdered sugar, lemon zest, and vanilla until smooth. Spoon into a pastry bag fitted with a ¼-inch tip. Hold a cannoli shell in one hand; with the other, pipe filling halfway into the shell. Turn the shell around and fill the other side. Repeat with the remaining shells and filling.

Arrange on a platter and dust with cocoa powder or powdered sugar. Decorate ends of cannoli if desired with chopped pistachios, mini chocolate chips, or candied fruit. Serve cannoli immediately.

Serves 4-6

Papà Paolo's Tiramisu

As far back as we can remember, we always watched our Papà Paolo make this recipe. We have the most beautiful memories of eating this dessert with him when we were kids. Our Papà is our role model and everything we want to be as men when we grow up. He is our best friend, has provided for us and our family, and has shown us what it is to be a husband and father. Family is everything. Tiramisu, which translates to "pick me up," is a popular coffee-flavored Italian dessert, rich, creamy, and infused with marsala wine. Our family recipe uses no eggs—yes, we said no eggs—and it is the best. Grazie, Papà!

1 cup brewed Italian espresso
Marsala wine
3 cups mascarpone
1½ cups condensed milk
Ladyfingers
Cocoa powder

Pour the espresso into a shallow dish, and allow to cool. When cool, add the marsala wine. The amount of marsala wine depends on how strong you want that flavor to be. We add a good splash, as we love the taste.

In a large bowl, whisk the mascarpone and condensed milk together until thick and free of lumps. You don't want it to be runny. The mixture should be as smooth and silky as us!

Now briefly soak the ladyfingers in the espresso and marsala mixture. Turn them a couple of times so they are nicely coated but not soggy. They should absorb the mixture and take on a pale coffee color but remain firm.

Cover the bottom of a large serving bowl—we like to use a clear glass bowl, to show off the different layers of the tiramisu—with a layer of ladyfingers. Spoon on some of the mascarpone mixture, and smooth it over the top and to the edges of the bowl.

Now sprinkle cocoa powder over the top. Make sure to cover all the mascarpone mixture—don't be shy with the amount of cocoa you use. Now repeat this process until all the ladyfingers and mascarpone mixture are used. You should have 3-4 layers, ending with the mascarpone mixture and cocoa powder.

Cover with plastic wrap, and chill in the fridge overnight. It will be perfect for serving the next day and enjoying with the whole family.

Serves 4-6

Finale

    We hope we have inspired you to cook Italian at home, eat together as a family, and pass on the love, tradition, and passion of cooking and food to your family and friends. Remember, love makes the world go round . . . but Italians make it worth the trip! We have no doubt that everything you make will be Twintastico.

Yours Twincerely,
The Alberti Twins
xxxx

Index

Addictive Anchovy and Sage Fritti, 31
Aioli Dip, 35
Alberti's Amazing Almond Muffins, 189
Alberti's Amazing Italian Burgerlicious Burger, 157
Alberti's Arancini Golden Italian Balls, 41
Alberti's Nutcracker, 191

Babbo's Biscotti, 195
Bella Broad Bean Dip, 23
Big Cannoli, The, 201
Biggest and Best Italian Sandwich in the World, The, 139
Blessed Basil Pesto, 25

Caesar Salad, 49
Catchy Cacio e Pepe, 87
Cheeky Chestnut Cake, 169
Cheesiest, Creamiest, Dreamiest Mac and Cheese Ever!, The, 97
Classic Carbonara, 117
Crunchy Crostini, 53

Fabulicious Farro, 45
Fancy Figs, 75
Fantastico Calamari Fritti, 39
Figtastic Summer Salad, 47
Forza Four-Cheese Lasagna, 85
Frittata, La, 65

Gnocchi con Pollo e Funghi, 95

Gorgeous Gnocchi, 93

Holy Focaccia, 55

Italian Almond Cheesecake, 183
Italian Bangers and Mash, 147
Italian Eggs Benedict, 63
Italian Fish and Chips, 137
Italian Roast, 141
Italian Shepherd's Pie, 159
Italian Stallion Pasta Bake, 103
Italian Tacos, 153
Italian Yorkshire Puddings, 155
Italia's Creamy Cannellini Dip, 29

Lemon Linguine, 83
Luscious Lemon Ricotta Cake, 175

Magnifico Melanzane, 105
Mamma Mia Marinara Sauce, 27
Mamma's Spaghetti al Pomodoro, 123

Naughty Nutella Pancakes, 199
Nonna Maria's Chicken Cutlets, 127
Nonna's Tortellini en Brodo, 69
Nutty Nutella Cheesecake, 185

Olive Oil Cake, 173
Our Big and Bouncy Bomboloni Italian Balls, 187

Pane di Patate, 57
Pane Toscano, 59
Panna Cotta con Frutti di Bosco, 193
Papà Paolo's Tiramisu, 203
Passionate Penne all'Arrabbiata, 77
Pasta e Fagioli, 73
Perfetto Penne alla Vodka, 99
Perfetto Polenta Cake, 179
Pesce Pesce, 133
Piccoli Cuscini, 51
Polenta Fries with Aioli Dip, 35
Pollo al Marsala, 131
Porky Porchetta, 161
Pretty Polenta Crostini, 37

Racy Rigatoni, 91
Ravishing Risotto Verde, 115
Regina Margherita Pizza, 151
Risotto ai Funghi, 113
Romantic Ricotta Balls, 197

Salmon with a Pistachio, Honey, and Herb Crust, 135
Sassy Stromboli, 149
Saucy Spaghetti alla Puttanesca, 89
Seductive Saltimbocca, 129
Sexy Spirali Pasta, 101
Spaghetti Aglio, Olio, e Peperoncino, 81
Spaghetti alle Vongole, 121
Spaghetti and Meatballs, 79

Spaghetti con Frutti di Mare, 119
Spectacular Spinach and Ricotta Ravioli, 107
Spezzatino di Manzo con Polenta, 143

Tantalizing Tagliatelle with Italian Sausage in a
    Creamy Leek Sauce, 109
Tasty Tomato and Basil Soup, 67

Torta Caprese, 177
Torta della Nonna, 181
Torta di Limoncello, 167
Torta di Nocciole, 171
Tuscan bread, 59
Tuscan Crostini with Chicken Liver Pâté, 43
Twillionaire's Shortbread, 165

Twinning Tuscan Vegetable Soup, 71
Twintastico Italian Sausage-in-the-Hole with a
    Racy Red Wine Sauce, 145
Twintastico Tagliatelle al Ragu, 111

Zucchini Fritti, 33